Make It Happen

Rob Friedman
With Malcolm J. Nicholl

Commonsense Tips for Business Success from
the Co-Founder of an Internet Company that's
Sold $37 Billion of Real Estate

First Edition

TABLE OF CONTENTS

Introduction

I believe in the American way and the American dream. We're blessed to live in the greatest country in the world.

I've written this book because I want to encourage the spirit of entrepreneurism. I want to help give people the confidence to take that next step to go out and start a business, create a lot of jobs, and make a lot of money. I want to continue to help make the United States the greatest country in the world.

In my entrepreneurial life I've launched many businesses, starting at a very early age. I've always had an intense, burning passion to succeed in business. That's just who I am. I've had some big hits and I've had some misses. I'm fortunate to have helped create and develop Ten-X and Auction.com, the country's leading online real estate endeavor that's sold over $37 billion worth of properties. (Although, I have to honestly give most of the credit to my long-term friend and business partner, Jeff Frieden, and our incredible colleagues).

I'm also honored to have been named Internet Person of the Year by the Internet Marketing Association join previous honorees such as Mark Zuckerberg of Facebook; Tony Hsieh, CEO of Zappos; and Justin Choi, founder of Nativo.

My original goal when I first started jotting down the notes for this book was to produce a guide for my children, my nieces and nephews, and their children. My thinking was simply to share with them the basic tenets that have been partially responsible for helping make me a business success.

But as I discussed the book with my son and a few friends they asked me to open up about some of my personal business experiences from which I've learned so much. So that's what I've done.

The book was never intended to be an intellectual masterpiece with new cutting edge business processes—and it's not. But I believe you'll find plenty of good, yet simple, foundational business practices that are really important for almost any business—practical, commonsense business-building tips. Maybe some of them will be familiar to you and the content of this book will serve as positive reinforcement to what you're already doing—or what know you should be doing. On the other hand, I'm sure you'll discover some strategies that you'll immediately recognize as ways to dynamically grow your own business.

I also want to say a word about giving back to the community. Frankly, although I'm deeply appreciative of my business success, I get just as much satisfaction—maybe even more—by being able to give back, not only financially but also through contributing my time, talents and energy to causes like Big Brothers Big Sisters and other children's educational charities around the world. I encourage you to give back, too.

America is still genuinely the land of opportunity. It is for everyone who embraces the concept of working hard and working honestly as the means of achieving entrepreneurial fulfillment. I truly believe that in order keep America strong we need good responsible entrepreneurs to create jobs. I trust you will learn from my experiences and chart your own course to business success and worthwhile philanthropy.

Chapter 1. An Entrepreneur Is Born

Entrepreneurship and real estate. It's in my DNA. As far back as I can remember I was interested in doing deals and making a profit—and having fun at the same time.

From an early age I was lucky to have had two great mentors, my mother and my grandmother. My mother has been an extremely positive and motivational influence on my life. She has been a true go-getter; very supportive; always there for me.

My grandmother was a hands-on business person, constantly regaling me with stories of my great-grandfather and of the deals they did; how they made money buying and selling real estate. It really captured my young imagination. It really intrigued me.

Think about it: My grandmother was a business success—back in the 1940s and 1950s when it was not the norm for a woman. She was divorced (also not common at the time) and doted on her four grandsons. When I was little she'd take us to look at the land she owned out in the middle of nowhere—out in the desert. I remember riding around with her while she told us how she had bought the land at an auction with her father, a retired dentist, and would then sell it, and carry back paper. In other words, she would carry the financing on the property.

She owned land throughout southern California, mostly in rural areas which became much more valuable as the population grew and expanded. One specific purchase that comes to my mind is a raw piece of land in the desert. I believe she paid less than $1,000 for a 40-acre parcel and ultimately sold it 25 years later for over $500,000. It happened to be near Palm Springs!

I always enjoyed looking at land with my grandmother. She was smart enough to make each trip an adventure and not only keep a youngster interested, but also excited. I didn't realize it at the time, of course, but she was definitely grooming me to be the entrepreneur that I am today. One piece of advice she gave me, that has stayed with me and is a philosophy with which I wholeheartedly agree: when you have a bona fide buyer for your land… SELL.

My grandmother knew what she was doing. She never wanted for anything, but she never lived beyond her means. She was always humble about her success. She lived a good life for a long time and her real estate investments funded her retirement.

The Lure of Garage Sales

So, my grandmother made me aware of the power of making a profit and the value of doing the right kind of deals. That interest manifested itself in other ways when I was very young. Indelibly printed in my mind is a passion for garage sales. There was one day—I couldn't have been more than seven or eight years old—when I was riding my Schwinn bike in our Anaheim neighborhood and a garage sale grabbed my attention. I was fascinated by all of the stuff that was up for sale. But what really caught my eye was a fantastic set of slot cars. These were little motorized cars that you would race on tracks. You'd control them with a gun-like trigger. You could buy different motors and different tires. It was a very popular hobby at the time and, frankly, quite expensive.

I stared in astonishment at this set of three or four cars with multiple motors, tracks, wheels, tires and controls.

There was no doubt in my mind that someone had spent $300.00 on this set. I guessed that it had belonged to the son of the lady who was selling them and that he must have outgrown them. But what really mattered to me was that I was able to buy the lot for $2.00. I will never forget it. I bought something that cost $300.00 for just $2.00. There was so much stuff I had to ride my bike back and forth two or three times to get it all home.

I had a ton of fun playing with that set, all the while knowing that I could make a profit if I wanted to resell it. I reckoned I could easily make 10 times what I'd paid for it. I couldn't believe it. But beyond the thought of profit, those slot cars gave me years of enjoyment. So, I guess it's true that one man's trash is another man's treasure.

I totally got a kick out of the garage sales. It was a way to make my allowance go further and there was always the thrill of finding something valuable for next to nothing and doing the deal. It was probably no great surprise that I also got into holding sales of my own to raise extra cash.

I was good with numbers. I was good at spotting an opportunity. When I was about nine years old I went to a fair at the local church, St. Justin's. They had a large, homemade, and very rudimentary roulette wheel, and you could use your ride tickets to place a bet. I quickly figured out that one of the spots on the wheel had the wrong odds —odds that favored the player (in this case me). I'm afraid I took the house (the church) to the cleaners because they were letting us sell the ride tickets back to them. I also confess that I returned in the afternoon to try my luck again —but by then they had corrected their mistake.

During these formative years garage sales continued to be a part of my life. I always seemed to be able to spot a good deal. And I was having fun. When I was older—probably around 11 or 12—I saw some jewelry at one garage sale. I wasn't an expert on jewelry, of course, but it looked like the quality of some of the items my grandmother wore and I knew she didn't have cheap stuff. I paid about $2.00 for it and, sure enough, it turned out to be 14k gold.

I guess I was into everything. Like many young kids of my age I also—for a while—had a paper route. It only lasted a few months because I could never get enough sleep. I was so conscientious I'd be awake half the night worrying about making sure I got up on time for the early morning deliveries. I'd do anything to earn extra money. But I didn't think of it as work. I enjoyed it all.

Lessons Learned

What did I learn from those early days? Looking back I've come to appreciate that my grandmother was a particular role model and mentor. But my mother also planted the seeds of business in my mind and really nurtured my entrepreneurial spirit. If you're not lucky enough to have a mentor like them, try and find one. I will write much more on this subject later in the book.

Among the other early lessons I acquired in my formative years was that a) money is made in the buy and b) you've not only got to be in the right place at the right time, but have the courage to act on it.

What do I mean by making money in the buy? Obviously, if you buy a $300.00 item for $2.00 you know you're going to make money. But if you buy a $200.00 item for $300.00 I don't care how good that $200.00 item is, you're going to lose money because you overpaid from the beginning. The profit in any deal, whether it's real estate or any other transaction, is typically made at the initial deal. When you get liquid again is when you sell, but the profit is made the day you buy. It's one of the easiest things to do in business. Today, with the Internet, it's remarkably simple to educate yourself about the true worth of anything and to make money in the buy. Buy wholesale; there's no reason to pay retail. I truly believe in the old adage that a dollar saved is a dollar earned.

If you recognize that you're in the right place at the right time and you have a little bit of money—be ready to act. That's what I did when I bought the slot car set. In this situation there was a lady with a lot of stuff in her garage and she didn't really want to deal with it. She wanted it gone, so she sold it to me for virtually nothing. I was in a position of advantage. If you want to be successful you have to take advantage of opportunity when you see it.

You can buy the nicest diamond in the world but if you pay too much for it be prepared to lose money if the day comes when you want to sell it. If you're knowledgeable and know the true worth, however, you'll typically make money. Similarly, if you're going to buy a building you've got to make sure the price is right. Do your research. When it came to buying the garage sale jewelry I guess I was semi-educated, but I also had the guts to make the decision. It was easy for me to make money on that one, too, because I got such a great deal in the buy.

So, let me reiterate: Educate yourself. Keep your eyes open. Be in the right place at the right time and act. These are messages you will continue to read in the next chapter and the ones that follow.

Chapter 2. The Teenage "Tycoon"

I had a keen eye for opportunity. I was always looking for a new deal. The mentoring from my grandmother and my own venture into the world of garage sales had given me a lust for business.

When I was about 12 or 13 and in the boy scouts I saw an ad in the back of Boys Life magazine offering to ship fireworks—firecrackers and bottle rockets—from the mid-west to California. I'm not even sure it was legal (it probably wasn't!) but I bought cases of stuff and made a lot of money selling them to all of my friends. That was another fun endeavor, although I don't know if my parents and neighbors appreciated it.

At about the age of 15 I got a part-time job for a little while doing phone sales. What an experience that was. My neighbor owned the business—a small call center, not more than half a dozen people. I'd go there in the evenings and at weekends and I'd phone people offering them a free charge card at Sears, Montgomery-Ward or J.C. Penney. I like to say it was my first and last true job; in other words, the only time when I was on someone else's payroll. The pay was minimal. But that's not a complaint. We made most of our money on commission and it was a pretty easy job. It taught me how to be nice to people, and how to handle rejection. It also gave me an appreciation of earning higher commissions—the harder I worked and the more accomplished I became, the more money I made.

Another great venture was buying and selling cars, which I did with my older brother Walter. He was really into cars and, in fact, had encouraged me to take auto shop as an elective at school. We'd get up early and look in the paper to see what cars were being advertised. We'd mostly buy old Camaros, Mustangs and Volkswagens and we'd fix them up and resell them. I wasn't even old enough to have a driving license when we did the first deal for a 1964 El Camino.

Swap Meets

It was also when I was about 15 years old that I started going to swap meets. If you don't know what a swap meet is—it's basically a flea market where people sell all kinds of stuff. There were quite a few flea markets in Orange County back then, especially at the old drive-in movie theaters and fairgrounds. I got little jobs helping people set up or take down their wares.

Then I progressed to selling stuff myself. Nothing special. Odds and ends like Christmas ornaments and plastic hangers. I was still in high school and I was making money. And that was great. Then I had the good fortune to meet Jeff Frieden who was selling stereo equipment and I thought, wow, this is much better than what I'm doing. Fortunately, he was a cool guy who kindly showed me where he was buying his merchandise in downtown Los Angeles. So I bought a van and got into the stereo business. (I was always good about saving money and I'd saved enough money from my other ventures to be able to afford it. I'd opened a bank account when I was really young. It was fun watching the balance get bigger!)

There were about half a dozen swap meets every weekend and I obviously couldn't handle them all myself so I hired my buddies to do them for me. I was 17 years old and making $300 to $500 a weekend. We'd kick back listening to music, drinking the beer that we'd brought in our Playmate coolers, selling stereo equipment—and making money. It was a beautiful thing. We were teenage kids. We were out there having fun and doing a lot of deals.

It was another great learning experience. I was doing business with people of all races, religions and ages. The most important thing for me was to get out there and not be afraid to make mistakes and, most importantly, learn from those mistakes. In that environment I was able to make a lot of mistakes, and learn a lot more. One of the lessons I learned was that there are righteous people and there are jerks in all walks of life. Religion and race and age have nothing to do with it.

Jeff Frieden and I went to the same high school— Anaheim's Loara High. We went to the same football games, the same rock concerts, and the same swap meets. We had like-kind interests and really hit it off. I was crazy. He was crazier. It was the start of a business partnership that I'm proud to say endures today.

Smog Shop

After swap meets came my first real business venture— smog shops—which was thanks in large part to my older brother, Walter. In the state of California you have to get a smog inspection for your car at a licensed facility. At the time it was called Hamilton Test Systems. They would put your car on a dynamometer—where the wheels turn but you don't go anywhere—and test the smog emission. If the car fails you have to get it fixed at a licensed repair shop, a Class A VIP Smog repair shop.

Walter had had the brilliant idea of opening up a smog repair shop near the inspection facility closest to our home in Orange County. He had to take a test to become licensed. From the very first day my brother had people handing out flyers to drivers leaving the inspection place. If they had failed they were directed to Walter's place just down the street.

Most people want to get their cars repaired as fast as possible, and he was fulfilling that need. He had a captive audience from day one. People whose cars had failed would be driving out scratching their heads wondering where they were going to get their car fixed. And right in their face was someone with a flyer and a convenient solution: their car could be repaired and they'd be back in line in 30 minutes. Walter was in the right place at the right time to fulfill people's need. Business boomed from the moment he opened his doors.

As I mentioned earlier, at high school I'd had the opportunity to take an elective and—encouraged by my brother—I had picked Auto Shop purely and simply because it was a hobby of his. Walter had that kind of influence over me. When I was in the ninth grade he'd talked me into taking the class called Small Engines. From it, I learned to appreciate mechanics and enjoyed being able to understand how a lawn mower engine (a good ol' Briggs and Stratton) actually worked and how to make my minibike go faster.

Auto Shop was taught by Ted Brown, and it was an enthralling part of my week. It was great to discover the finer aspects of the internal combustion engine and what makes cars tick. In two years I learned how to be a mechanic. I wasn't the best mechanic in the world, by any means, but I learned enough to get by. In Auto Shop I met students who, based on the standards of most teachers, wouldn't cut the mustard. They were great guys, though, who desperately wanted to learn how to turn a wrench and eventually get a good job—and maybe even open an auto shop one day, ultimately creating jobs for others. While most of them were smart enough to graduate, some never did simply because they didn't see the benefit of being taught or should I say, force fed, a curriculum of classes that they had absolutely no interest in.

Unlike them I had more of a focus on academics. I had to. My father was a physician and my mother was a teacher and their mission was to guide me toward college so I duly took algebra, geometry, biology and the rest of the academic curriculum. I went on to graduate from high school with respectable grades, but I felt that I'd learned very little from the academics classes. Mr. Brown's Auto Shop was a different matter. (More on the subject of education later).

So, after graduating and beginning to take business classes at junior college I put my auto knowledge to good use combined with the knowledge I'd gained by watching the success of my brother Walter, a superb role model. And I out-and-out copied what he'd been doing with the smog test business. I took the test, got my license as a "Class A VIP Mechanic," and started my own company: Performance Tune-Up & Smog. Not in direct competition with my brother, of course. Instead, I deliberately looked for the busiest inspection facility in the state—which turned out to be in Los Angeles. And following Walter's example I rented a place as close to it as possible. It was basically not much more than a shack and, unfortunately, it was in a rough part of town.

The first day I was there, even before I'd opened shop, I had one of the most frightening experiences of my life. I got held up at gunpoint and my gold chain was ripped off my neck. A guy had driven up and leaned out of his car asking if I wanted to buy a gun—a gun which he was

actually waving around! It all happened so fast I didn't
have time to think. As I was talking to him he suddenly
grabbed the chain from my neck, a chain that had been
given to me by my grandmother. My instinctive reaction
was pretty stupid—because I fought back. He's driving off
down the street. I jump on him. I'm half in and half out of
the window with my arms around his neck trying to force
him to stop. And he's still got the gun in his hand struggling
to point it at me.

What the hell was I doing? It probably didn't take more
than 10 to 15 seconds before I came to my senses, realized
I was being stupid, and jumped out. I got all scuffed up,
tore my clothes, and had a few bruises. No serious physical
injury, but I was mentally scarred more than anything else.
To be honest, it was a traumatic experience. I'm sure it took
me six months to get over it and to this day I have a lot of
empathy for victims of violent crime. Of course, I called
the police to report the robbery and assault but they were so
busy with more important stuff they didn't even bother to
take a report.

Although I was shaken up I wasn't going to let that
assault stop me. The excitement over starting my new
business overrode my fears. I was determined to make it
work so, for protection, I got myself a Doberman and
carried a loaded gun. Every morning, for a while, I would
arrive at the smog shop to find my building covered in
graffiti. Solution: I always had a bucket of paint at hand
and immediately painted right over it. I just persevered.
Eventually the taggers got wise and gave up.

I also got to know the guys in the Latino and Black gangs.
They would come by every Friday and hit me up for
enough bucks to buy a case of beer. We had a pretty cool
relationship actually and, apart from that first day, I never

had any problems. They were just guys. And I've found that when you treat any human being with respect, typically you'll get along.

Like my brother before me, the smog shop was an instant success. I was swamped the first day and I went on to open a second smog repair shop on the other side of the inspection center. I was doing great. I was 18 years old and handling 30 repairs a day at $30 a piece. I was making good money.

At the same time I still had the swap meets going. I bought extra vans and hired friends to work the swap meets for me. They'd come to my house early in the morning and I'd load them up with the goods. And away they'd go.

My entrepreneurial life was taking off. I was juggling these different endeavors and they really needed my full-time attention. But I was also still at college—in second year of business school at Cypress Junior College. My dad had always instilled in his four sons the need to get a good education. What would he have to say?

I presented my dilemma to him, and he was open-minded enough to tell me, "OK. When your business slows down you go back to school." So, one of these days I'm going to go back to school!

Seriously, I'm a huge proponent of a good, solid education for all of our kids. It's the most important foundation in life. It just so happened that for me I was able to get hands-on learning and never looked back.

The smog shop business, however, wasn't destined to last. The state of California changed the law so that a smog repair shop could be run by anyone with the right equipment. I'd lost my competitive advantage and so after two years I was out of business.

By the way, I'd started cautiously and had only taken a month-to-month lease on the "shack." Once the landlord saw how successful my business had become he jacked up the rent. It was a great location—but as I had not felt able to commit to a longer term lease it had created extra overhead. Regardless, this was an incredible experience and a springboard to my next business. Luckily, I'd saved much of the money I'd made and was ready for the next opportunity.

If it seemed like I had the Midas touch I was soon to get a shock. I got into the jewelry business and it was a total flop. I rented a little kiosk in a shopping area right across from Disneyland and tried to sell jewelry that I'd bought wholesale in L.A.'s jewelry district. I didn't know much about jewelry and it never took off. It wasn't one of my best ideas and my assessment, on reflection, was that I probably had more guts than brains.

I then made a bad investment in a Hawaii land deal with a friend of my mom's. We should have known better. It was a pie in the sky deal. And what did we know about land in Hawaii? Until you have a lot of money and you've surrounded yourself with people you really respect who are going to vet deals for you it's more sensible to have personal knowledge of where you're putting your hard-earned dollars. The Hawaii guys weren't criminals—just bad operators who got greedy. At one point they had a dynamite opportunity to sell the land at a wonderful profit but they believed that a big developer would come along and buy at a higher price. Then the market nosedived!

So, I had a few losers during this stage of my life. But my attitude was that you just have to keep going for it—until you get a winner. No-one bats 1000 percent. You simply try and try again.

Lessons Learned

What did I learn in my teenage years?

- Don't be too proud to copy a great idea—and improve on it. My brother was the pioneer. I simply grew the same kind of business in a better location. It's never a bad idea to learn from a great idea as long as you're ethical and legal about it. If you see success, copy it. Learn from the successes of the pioneers; learn from their mistakes, too.

- Location is important.

- See a need and fill a need.

- Find great partners.

- Learn how to get along with people.

More on all of these lessons in later chapters.

Chapter 3. Partnering with Jeff

From swap meets to stereo stores! My good friend, Jeff Frieden, who'd been my partner at the swap meets and had introduced me to selling stereos, was working as a salesman for a group of guys who'd successfully launched some huge discount stereo stores in L.A. Later we discovered that they were part of the Israeli mafia. They'd acquired products at huge discounts, and sold them, but had never actually paid for them. That was a lesson in how not to do business that we would never dream of emulating.

But before we knew that their business was not being run ethically I spotted that there was a golden opportunity. There weren't any similar stores in Orange County that sold lower-priced, good value stereos. So I proposed to Jeff that we open the first. This was before Federated, before Circuit City, before the Good Guys. So, in December, 1983 we opened our own store called Stereo Connection with a big advertising campaign. We basically took what we'd learned from selling at the swap meets and transferred that know-how into a retail location.

It worked. We sold out the first day and had to rush back to L.A. to buy more merchandise. It was an itty bitty store; no more than 1,500 sq ft, but it was pretty exciting for a couple of young guys. Sales continued to be brisk and we built Stereo Connection into a small chain of five stores throughout Orange County.

One of the ways we grew the business was by offering a very clever loss leader—the Pen Watch. It was a nice little steel pen with a built-in watch. They cost us $2.05 and we'd advertise in the paper and sell them for $1.99. So, yes, we were losing money on each one we sold—but every morning we'd have people lining up to buy them. It was the greatest little loss leader in the world. We sold thousands of those pen watches and some of these folks, of course, didn't just buy the pen watches. Once we had them inside the door they ended up purchasing much bigger ticket items, so it proved to be an incredible promotion.

In many ways Stereo Connection was a great training ground for retail experience. I learned how to be a merchant, a retailer, how to buy and finance the merchandise, how to floor the merchandise. Flooring is when a manufacturer sells merchandise to a flooring company (basically a finance company) on behalf of the retailer so that the retailer can carry a bigger inventory and bigger selection of goods than he would otherwise be able to afford. The retailer, of course, pays finance charges—it could be about 1 percent a month (12 percent year)—but is able to sell more products and build up his creditworthiness in the process. So, it's worthwhile.

One interesting situation arose when I was 21 years old. It was just before Christmas—our busiest time of the year. We'd do as much business in December as we would the rest of the year. I placed a huge order, somewhere in the region of $200,000 to $300,000 with Tatung, who made good quality televisions. But my age worked against me. Even though we'd done a tremendous amount of business with them over the previous two years and had an impeccable credit history they declined to ship such a big order because I was so young. I'd wanted Tatung because their TVs were really high quality and higher priced and I could have made more money selling them.

Tatung, however, didn't want to take the risk. But it was their loss. Unfortunately, it was their sales guy's loss as well. I remember their representative, Nick Palazola, who was a really good guy, literally crying because of his lost commission. But I desperately needed merchandise for Christmas and there was no way I was going to be thwarted so I called my buddy, Barry, at Sohnen Enterprises and bought more Sharp products instead. They shipped to me the next day and I sold it all. I made money and they made money because they didn't have a hang-up about my age and they trusted me.

The stereo business was a superb education and an incredible stepping stone. Like the swap meet business you deal with people of every race and culture and I discovered that in every race and culture there are ethical people and unethical people. You just need to be able to differentiate.

First Auction

While we were running the stereo stores I heard about a guy called Bob Hamel who was a stereo auctioneer. His specialty was coming into stores and auctioning scratched or dented out-of-the-box type merchandise, the kind of stuff that's hard to sell. I decided it had to be worth a shot and brought him in. I'd had a couple of experiences with auctions with my grandmother. When I was 11 years old she'd taken me to a furniture auction—some guys were liquidating a business—and bought a nice secretary desk for my bedroom. I was fascinated by the showmanship of the event and also remember thinking that she'd paid too much for it. My grandmother also took me to a jewelry auction where she bought a little ring for herself. I didn't know whether that was a deal or not! But auctions seemed to work for furniture and jewelry. Why not stereos?

I ran big newspaper ads similar to those I would normally place for a major sale event except that the headline screamed: AUCTION. It was amazing. It generated three times our normal traffic. There were people lined up all the way down the street waiting to get in. Between Friday night and Sunday we held four auctions and it was standing room only. I was on stage holding up merchandise as the auctioneer did his thing, thinking this was really something. We did more business that weekend than we would normally do in a month. We grossed about $100,000.

What a powerful way to sell a lot of merchandise fast. It was an 'aha' moment and opened my eyes to what I call seminar sales or mass marketing sales, where you're selling to a whole group of people rather than one-on-one. This was my first experience staging an auction. It was hyper sales and I realized I enjoyed it a whole lot more.

After four or five years, though, a Circuit City opened across the street from our 6,000 square foot Westminster outlet. We saw the writing on the wall. We were selling a commodity. The big boys could kill us on the pricing. It was time to move on. So we sold the stereo stores but kept the property. And that was probably the most important lesson from this undertaking. The store was a perfect location for retail—right on a signalized corner—and I had been able to buy the property. I'd really wanted that property and I'd hunted down the owner to make an offer on it. This was back when Jimmy Carter was president and interest rates were high—12 to 14 percent. As part of the deal I had to assume the 12¾ percent mortgage. But it was worth it and I managed to keep up the payments. To this day I still own that location. It has paid for itself three-and-a-half times over and is probably worth five times what I paid for it.

This was actually my second foray into property ownership. The first was a little triplex in a poor neighborhood of Anaheim. I quickly discovered that I didn't enjoy being a property manager and having to deal with tenants on the everyday issues. I didn't have the temperament for it and it didn't seem like an effective use of my time.

Lessons Learned

From my stereo business days I learned the power of staging auctions and the value of owning property. Earlier, my grandmother had taught me that owning land could be a phenomenal investment. Auctions. Land. Property. My destiny was falling into place.

Chapter 4. Going. Going. Gone.

I was hooked on the idea of auctions as a business model. It had made an immense impact on our stereo business. But I needed to know how to do it right. So I registered for auction school. It was a two-week course in Billings, Montana of all places—at the Western College of Auctioneering.

I was a southern California rock 'n' roll concert kind of guy; most of the other students were cowboys who had grown up on cattle ranches. I didn't know that real cowboys still existed but that's what they were and they planned on selling livestock. That, of course, was not what I had in mind! But they were a great group of guys and we got along famously. Together we picked up the singsong patter of an auctioneer practicing with brooms, pots and pans as the mock items up for sale.

When I got back home I began doing auctions on the side, pretty much selling anything and everything that I could. Stereos. Furniture. Cars. For experience I would make myself available to do any kind of auctioneering. I did a lot of charity auctions for free (and I still do) but it was tough getting gigs because most people naturally preferred more experienced auctioneers. I was lucky to have a couple of great mentors in the industry who let me get up on the block and do the auctioneering.

One of them was a wonderful older gentleman, named Phil Hanson, who was about 70 years old at the time. Phil ran auctions selling items that had been part of the displays in the model homes at the big William Lyon's developments. He sold everything from the furniture to the pots and pans. He would get the auctions under way, and after about five or 10 minutes he'd call me up to take over.

I would sell for an hour and then he would take over just to conclude the event. That was my first big break as an auctioneer. I was so blessed that he'd given me a chance and revealed some of the tricks of the trade. I met Phil as the result of a different business venture completely.

Artists' Colony

In the fall of 1986 I bought a two-storey brick building and a former fire station next door that were located in a not-so good part of Santa Ana.

The building, which nestled between the Diamond Ice Co. and the railroad tracks, had been constructed around 1937 and needed a lot of work—not only painting, paneling and other cosmetic repairs, but also to meet earthquake standards. I'd bought it for an amazingly low $10.00 a square foot. To most people it probably looked like it was not just a white elephant but also an old white elephant. I could see its potential, however, and my vision was to turn it an artists' haven.

And that's what I did. It became an artists' colony housing visual and performing artists, illustrators, graphic designers, advertising layout artists—all kinds of wonderfully creative people—in 22 studios. Because it was off the beaten path, I could offer artists a large space for pretty low rates. It was perfect for them. As an old building it had a certain aura and charm. A really cool vibe. Although I'm not an artist I considered fixing up old buildings my artistry. It gave me a lot of pleasure.

As it turned out the guy who sold me the building was an auction aficionado, who became a friend and introduced me to Phil Hanson.

Land Auctions

One day I saw an ad in the paper for a land auction and out of curiosity I went to check it out. The auction was crowded. I carefully observed how it was being staged and although it was obviously successful I wasn't overly impressed with the event. And it hit me. I knew how to do this business. I could do it better. I already knew how to buy land thanks to my grandmother's guidance. I already knew how to promote my own auctions thanks to the stereo store experience. I already knew how to be an auctioneer thanks to my time with the cowboys and Phil Hanson's kindness. I could pretty much figure out the rest.

So I decided to start my own land auction business with some financial backing from Jeff and other investors. It certainly wasn't an overnight endeavor. I knew that I had to have a sizeable number of properties to turn an auction into a worthwhile event so I spent a whole year slowly but surely assembling 200 parcels of land.

I was lucky in having a head start—thanks to my grandmother (again!). In her estate she'd left almost 50 lots and I was able to get my brothers to agree to let me sell them. The key way I acquired land, though, was to identify potential deals in the upper desert and semi-rural areas within an hour and a half of Los Angeles. I sent out letters to anyone who owned land; I went to tax sales. I'd done my homework so I knew exactly what the land was worth. I offered 100 percent cash and closing in 30 days. I made it really simple for the owners and for them it was a blessing because no-one had been promoting their land and they hadn't had an offer in years.

Then I went for it and held an auction in the ballroom of a major hotel. It was a monster success. A new business was launched! No-one else was making a market in inexpensive land.

Meanwhile, while I was assembling the land, Jeff had been running a Volkswagen dealership that we owned in La Habra. That came about because we got really good terms for commercial real estate that we wanted to buy—but had to take over the business at the same time.

But with the mega-success of the land auction I persuaded Jeff that we needed to work together to capitalize on it. Result: We went on to run land auctions for 10 years, acquiring land in many different ways: from private parties and from tax sales, for instance. Over time we became the market leader in the U.S. selling parcels of land that were worth under $50,000. Typically, this is the kind of land that owners have a hard time selling. Brokers aren't usually all that interested in handling them because the commission they can earn is so small, especially when you factor in their time and advertising costs.

What made us different was that we were able to mass market. We would send out thousands of postcards to potential sellers and buy their land for cash. When we would have enough properties we would heavily advertise on radio and in the newspapers and we'd send out brochures to people who expressed interest in buying. We always strongly encouraged them to go and take a look at the properties because an informed buyer is much better equipped to make a smart decision and likely to be a happier buyer. And they'd typically pay more.

Then we'd stage one big auction event and we'd always stress that if people hadn't looked at the property they shouldn't bid. We'd also carry the financing—low money down, easy financing—so we were making profit on that aspect, too. We gave people credit with 15 to 20 percent down.

We'd buy anything big enough that wasn't in the flood plain. I'll be very frank. Some of the land was beautiful; some if it was on the side of a mountain. But you never know what's going to appeal to someone or what use they have in mind. Perhaps they want to build a cabin or camp out there or ride their motorcycle or look for rocks? You never know.

It was a very, very good business and the next stepping stone in my career.

Research "Down Under"

The logical business progression was to move from land into real estate property. And we needed an education. So Jeff and I did something most people might find a little unusual. In 1989 we jumped on a plane to Australia and New Zealand where real estate auctions were commonplace.

We didn't have any contacts. We didn't really know what we were doing. But we figured out that the Aussies and the Kiwis were the experts, so "down under" was the place to go. We went for two weeks and as soon as we arrived we got out the yellow pages, looked up all of the major real estate auction companies, and went and knocked on their doors. We'd just tell them that we'd come over from the states to learn the business and asked if they could help us.

It was amazing how they embraced us. Between the two countries we probably had 15 different meetings. We sat there like good students at the feet of guys who had been working the business for a long time. They freely gave us all the ins and outs of the real estate auction world. We learned from their successes and from their failures. By the time we left we had made a lot of good friends and we understood the business pretty darn well. Subsequently, any time we had a question we had someone to call, someone to mentor us. In fact, one of the guys, Keith Jones, came over to the states to help us with one of our first auctions.

Of course, these auction guys knew that we weren't going to compete with them in Australia and New Zealand. After all we'd come halfway across the world. And they accepted that we were just nice young guys who were simply there to learn. Nevertheless, it was remarkable that they were so open in revealing the secrets and tricks of the trade. Some of them even gave us their training manuals. They were ' that kind to us because we'd traveled a long way, we didn't have big egos, and we were very open to learning. We were so thankful that they were gracious enough to help us. It would probably have taken us years—if ever—to gain the knowledge that we gained in those two weeks.

You can do the same kind of thing for pretty much any kind of business. But you've got to be willing to ask. You've got to have the guts to go to the experts. If you're thinking of starting a business you can now get on Google and search for people in the same type of business in other states and ask them for their help. What kind of advertising, what kind of promotions do they do? Copy success. Figure out what doesn't work. Talk to as many successful people in that industry as you can, keep asking questions, and take copious notes. And you'll be amazed how quickly you can learn a business.

You don't need to blaze the trail. The trail has already been blazed for you. All you need to do is get on the Internet and find other people elsewhere that are in the same business. It's obviously easier if they are out of state and know that you're not going to be fighting for the same customers. So, just call them. Be upfront. Tell them, "I'm from out of state. I'm just starting my business. Can I ask you a few questions?"

Make as many calls as you can and you'll unearth some really cool people willing to share their information with you. This will cut the learning curve tremendously. So many people are afraid to ask. My advice and I can't say it often enough: Just ask and you'll be surprised how many people in this great country of ours are willing to help. Especially when you're a start-up. You can even ask if you can buy their training manual. Sometimes they will say yes, sometimes no, and sometimes they will just give it to you. But you won't know until you ask.

Home Auctions

Our big break—our expansion from selling land to selling property—came when a major Inland Empire developer, Charles Ware, owner of Aware Development Company, asked us to auction homes he was having difficulty selling after the housing market crash of 1990. He basically came to us and said, "Hey, I really like what you guys are doing with your land auction business, would you consider doing a home auction for us?"

At the time I was working out of my artists' colony building in Santa Ana. I'd go to work in a tank top and shorts, get there at 10:00 a.m., leave at 2:00 p.m., arranging the land auction deals. It was a great life. And so when Charles approached me about doing home auctions in all honesty my initial reaction was, "I don't know, man. That sounds like a lot of work."

But Jeff who's a workaholic (and, as I mentioned, truthfully the guy who built Auction.com) said, "Yeah, of course we're going to do it."

We agreed with Charles, who's a really great guy, that we'd do the auction for 2 percent commission. Later we discovered we should have charged 5 percent but this was an invaluable foot in the door that could not be underestimated. We were happy to do it.

We set up the auction at the Riverside Convention Center and about a thousand people showed up. We sold 54 Moreno Valley homes in one day. $10 million in sales. And we made $200,000. That's the power of an auction. Charles was smart enough to see that the market was going down and he wanted to move his entire inventory and pay off the bank. Not only were we thankful for the deal but we were also thankful that he had listened to us and agreed to invest the necessary big bucks in advertising. It hadn't been easy. He already had an ad agency and when we had a meeting at his office they had their own ideas. We got into a big argument. I knew how to do radio and print and I insisted my strategy was the one to follow. Luckily he agreed and declared, "We're doing it Rob's way." He was a man of his word. He covered all the advertising costs and we kicked butt. He'd taken a chance on us and it paid off big-time.

He had also pushed us into an incredible new opportunity.

We set up a new business, Real Estate Disposition Corp. (REDC) and focused on selling foreclosed homes, excess builder inventory and commercial buildings. Jeff took the lead and the business boomed. We were running auctions all the time and had to hire several auctioneers. We made a point of hiring only the very best Hall of Fame auctioneers because our modus operandi was to always be top notch.

We aggressively advertised. Every which way imaginable. Print. Radio. Direct mail. Even cardboard bootleg signs on telegraph poles. Frankly, those signs were an eyesore (and probably illegal). But we were so single-mindedly focused on doing a superlative job for our clients that in the middle of the night we'd go out and attach 2,000 of them within a five-mile radius of a subdivision. We were willing to do whatever it took.

The signs worked. They attracted a lot of attention. Unfortunately, they also attracted the attention of the city attorney who threatened us with jail if he saw one more sign. As we didn't want to spend so much as a night behind bars we decided it was time to halt that particular advertising technique!

When the recession of the 1990s drew to a close the market for home auctions died down so we concentrated again on the land auction business…until the need was revived a decade later by another housing market crash.

As the business developed we joined forces with Impac Mortgage to sell the growing number of foreclosures in Southern California and staged giant auctions in hotel ballrooms and convention centers.

The first, at the Los Angeles Convention Center in May 2007, attracted more than 7,000 potential buyers bidding on 300 homes. We had two live auctions going on at the same time in something like 200,000 square feet of space—about the size of four supermarkets. It was so big the auctioneer couldn't even see the bidders at the back of the room. It was so crowded the fire marshal almost shut us down. The way we handled it was to break the properties down into blocks of 100 and only allow people in the room who wanted to bid on one of those 100 properties. To keep everyone happy while they waited for their property to come on the block we handed out $10.00 food vouchers.

As the recession deepened other lenders with excess inventory began using our services and the business boomed.

But the move that was to propel our company into the stratosphere was a move with the times—into the burgeoning world of online marketing.

Chapter 5. Auction.com

Sometimes when you're in the right place at the right time; when you've had the right experience and have built the right reputation; that's when incredible opportunities come right to your door.

In 2006 a big client, a major financial institution, approached us and suggested that we put together an online auction for them. The business eventually became Auction.com and we've sold more than 100,000 properties worth more than $37 billion. In just eight years. We're expanding internationally and it's growing by the year.

When the client first came to us it was my partner Jeff, the eternal optimist, who didn't hesitate for a moment. Absolutely no problem, he told them. We'll have it done in a year. Then he called and told me. And it was my job to figure it out.

We needed to create a platform that gave the vibe of a live auction, like those we'd operated in hotel ballrooms, but have it happen online. Working with our partner, John Morrone, and his incredible team of developers we made it happen. Everything I'd learned from live auctions, everything that got people excited and help them make buying decisions, went into its creation.

We spent a couple hundred thousand dollars designing the software solution, which might sound like a lot but is a fraction of software designing costs today. Initially, we were doing it to make our client happy; we weren't even sure it was going to work. We kicked it off by putting 10 percent of our own properties on the site to test it out and lo and behold it worked. So we began to gradually add more and more properties.

Domain Name

One significant step in our growth was the purchase of the domain name, Auction.com. I knew it existed and had been keeping in touch with the owner for quite a while because I felt a name like that would be perfect branding and from a marketing view would put us over the top. Therefore, in March 2009, we bought it for almost $1.8 million. Yes, $1.8 million just for a domain name. But it was well worth it. It's an incredibly easy name for people to remember. And when you're spending more than $25 million a year in advertising we knew that it would pay for itself many times over. It was a domain name that was "worth its weight in gold."

We changed our company name, too, from Real Estate Deposition Corp (REDC) to Auction.com. It changed us from a company to a brand.

And we've never looked back.

We had a winning combination: a really great platform that got people excited about how they could buy and sell properties online coupled with an unforgettable domain name. The other dynamic element: partners. Jeff himself was amazing at persuading major financial institutions to use our system. And the guys at Stone Point Capital, the big private equity firm that had bought half of our company in November 2008, were instrumental in opening doors for him. To be honest I'd been reluctant to bring in partners. Jeff and I had never had partners before. I'd never had to be accountable to anyone, but Jeff really wanted to forge this relationship and I agreed. And we're growing larger than I'd ever imagined. There's tremendous synergy between us; we're all on board heading in the same direction and you can't beat working with people who know things you don't know.

The beauty of the online auction is its transparency. Nobody can game the system. Anybody who wants to bid can bid as long as they first prove their financial wherewithal. It's a huge development for the real estate business and its fair—and that's why government agencies use us now. We've increased distribution. We've broadened the market for both buyers and sellers. People across the globe can bid against each other.

Typically, in the past, it would be extremely difficult for someone in L.A. or San Francisco to find a property in Kansas City or Des Moines (or vice versa) because in these cities, as in thousands of others nationwide, everything would be handled by local brokers selling locally. Now people from all over the world can see properties from all over the world. We've helped tertiary markets sell properties they otherwise would not have been able to sell. We've helped the marketplace become efficient. And, as I mentioned, it's fair. I can't tell you how many people have come up to me and asked how they can get a deal on Auction.com. The fact of the matter is that everyone gets the same great deal.

As Auction.com expanded we brought in professional teams of marketers, and brilliant computer scientists and PhD's, and made the platform much better than our original version. But I'm proud to say the genesis and basic techniques are still the same—even today when we have a team of almost 1,000 associates in locations in California, Texas, Florida, and New York. The business continues to grow because we do a better job helping people buy and sell in a very expedient way.

The Online Process

How exactly does it work?

The listings come from numerous sources. Real estate agents, REITS, and large and small companies all post their properties. And, of course, lenders register their inventories of bank-owned foreclosures. It's a simple yet elegant virtual experience that, at the very least, helps narrow down buyers' search of desirable properties. They can also physically inspect the properties 30 days before the auction date. Just like the process in a traditional sale buyers have an opportunity to view properties that are to be sold online. In fact, I can't emphasize enough how important it is for someone to do that or have someone they trust do it for them; otherwise it's too much of a gamble.

Disclosure forms, sales contracts and everything you'd expect in an old-fashioned transaction are all available for download before a sale.

Potential buyers pay a deposit and must demonstrate that they are financially capable of covering their offer should they be the highest bidder. If they succeed they pay a "buyers premium" of 5 percent of the purchase price to compensate Auction.com for promoting and facilitating the auction. Agents acting on behalf of both buyer and seller can collect a commission and, as in almost every kind of auction, there is usually a reserve minimum set by the seller.

Have we really captured online the excitement of a live auction?

Here's what happens. People log on to their computer screens from their laptops—even their iPads and smartphones—and place their bids when the property in which they're interested goes on the bloc.

Bid after bid comes in and the screen flashes green with each new bid resetting the clock. As a deadline approaches the clock kicks into final countdown mode, for example … $250,000… $260,000… $270,000…$ 275,000…the latest bid is displayed on the screen. During the process the clock could be reset a couple of dozen times, or even more. Finally, "GOING ONCE" and "GOING TWICE" appears on the screen. "FINALIZING." The high bid: $280,000. Sold.

There could be 80 or more auctions of properties large and small all under way at any given time at our Irvine headquarters. Check out the Auction.com or Ten-X.com website and you'll see thousands of listings of properties that will be auctioned within the next 30 days. Last I just checked, there were 20,612. Those are homes. At the same moment there were 150 commercial buildings worth an estimated $700 million also up for sale. By the way, the most valuable property we've ever sold at auction was a $73.2 million office building in Glendale.

And people literally do participate in the auctions from all over the place. Recently one guy was bidding on a commercial property while vacationing on a cruise ship. He had his iPad and Wi-Fi connection and he was all set to participate.

Perhaps the ultimate seal of approval for Auction.com came in 2014 when Google identified us as one of the fastest growing companies with which they'd like to be involved and invested $50 million. That gave Auction.com a marketplace valuation of $1.2 billion. The Google guys have been wonderful mentors and, of course, when you have that level of quality and expertise backing the company it magnetically attracts other brilliant people to sit on the board or be advisors.

So, where do we go from here? Auction.com is undoubtedly the better mousetrap. Our goal is to be the real estate marketplace where everyone can buy and sell real estate efficiently. Agents, brokers, principals. Everyone. Our commercial division is now booming. We're expanding internationally. I have no doubt that we're going to continue to grow and grow. We're going to streamline the real estate industry worldwide.

That's been our experience. But what have I discovered along this journey that can assist you in your own endeavor? Staring with the next chapter I will provide some of those sound, commonsense tips I mentioned earlier.

Chapter 6. Make It Happen

"Make it happen" is a favorite expression of mine. Nike says, "Just do it." But I like to say, "Make it happen." If you adopt the attitude that you're going to make it happen, guess what? You make it happen.

So, what do you need to do to become a business success? Are there any "secrets?" Any shortcuts? Any "must-do's?" I've learned a lot during my career. And in this chapter I share some of the lessons with you.

Secrets? Not really.

Shortcuts? Absolutely not.

Must-dos? Absolutely. Positively.

So here are my recommendations. They're in no particular order except for the first—which is an absolute "must-do."

Work Hard

Perhaps this is a tip you don't want to hear? But there's no substitute for hard work, no matter how clever you are. Becoming successful is hard work and it requires 100 percent commitment.

It means working hard and getting the job done, whatever your job happens to be. If you're a dishwasher you have to be the best dishwasher there is—before you move up the ladder. Sadly—and I hate to say this—most people are lazy. They don't want to work, they don't want to think. To be successful you need an unwavering drive, a determination, a commitment.

You have to make the commitment to yourself.

You have to decide if you're willing to work 24/7 to achieve your goals. You have to decide what sacrifices you want to make when you're younger so that you can relish life when you're older. When I was a teenager working at the swap meets I used to get up at 5:00 a.m. on Saturday and Sunday mornings to go work and learn. No-one made me do it. It's what I wanted to do. I put work before pleasure. I wanted to make it happen. And I did.

Follow Your Dream

Do something you're passionate about. Do something you love. Do you like working on automobiles? Do you like working on computers? Are you interested in property? Are you good with your hands, with numbers, with words? You're good at something, but maybe you haven't figured it out yet.

One of the beautiful things about this world is that no two of us are alike. We all have different gifts, different skills, and different interests. Don't rush into something because you see dollar bill signs flashing. Before you start any kind of career or business make sure it's something you will enjoy; something that will make you want to jump out of bed in the morning. If you venture down the path of doing something that appeals to you from the get-go your chances of becoming proficient and successful are greatly enhanced. The laws of nature say that if you enjoy doing something, you're going to become good at it.

And guess what? If you're happy with your chosen vocation you're putting out a positive vibe to your customers. It's a winning atmosphere. Life is too short to try and make a living doing something that bores you or frustrates you. Sit down right now and seriously consider what will make you happy, what you will enjoy. And then you can take the rest of my advice and implement it to help you become the professional success you deserve to become. Do what you love and you will never work a day in your life.

I truly believe that each one of us has been given several gifts by the Almighty. Each of us has some talent or attribute. If we follow what we enjoy, and what comes naturally to us…if we pursue whatever gift we have been given…we can succeed. And success isn't always about the money.

I believe, for instance, that someone who wants to work with children and becomes a great teacher is a fantastic success. He or she is someone who makes a wonderful contribution to society. And that's a measure of success. Find your own gift and follow it with passion.

Fulfill a Need

You'll find a main path to success is to give people something that they want. Something that they need. Do they need the bread delivered earlier? Do they need transportation getting from one place to another? Do they need a piece of equipment repaired? Do they need a streamlined method to make a process easier? The list goes on and on.

As an entrepreneur you must identify other people's needs and figure out how to fulfill them or how to solve a problem that they have. I look at it like a puzzle. In my case I love putting together the pieces of a business deal. I always have my eyes open for opportunity. That's what I do. That's what I've always done.

As you discovered earlier, my first businesses ventures whether, for instance, the smog shop or the stereo shop, filled a need and filled a niche at the time. I used the money I made in those endeavors to purchase real estate and assets that basically paid me whether I worked or not (but that's another subject for later).

Daydream

I daydream.

I look at businesses and companies and I'm always analyzing what they're doing and what they could be doing better. I drive by a building and I study the signage, the décor, the landscaping and I consider—does it attract me? I look at a business that's demonstrably a winner and I think, how could I make it even better? Can I perfect that model or maybe take it to another area of the country? What can I do with a business that's successful in spite of its poor management?

I analyze everything. Are the employees polite? Did they greet me properly? Does the company have a great product? Is it an honest product? Is the design of the facility appealing? Would I return? Why wouldn't I return? Have they got the pricing right? Does the signage make sense? Is it the appropriate size for the building and type of business?

How good is their logo? I have two great friends who have built Monster Energy drink into a monster brand. They have a really distinctive green tear-shaped M logo on a black background. It's so iconic that people have it tattooed on their bodies or displayed on their motorcycle helmets. It's even recognized in countries where the drinks are not sold. Now that's what I call a logo. I'm sure it has contributed to their mega-success.

I never stop asking myself what could be done—even with my own businesses—to improve what we're doing for our customers.

I travel all over the world and I am constantly on the look-out for opportunities. I look for different ways that people are doing things. What can be done simpler? More affordably? I question everything. I don't have to come up with original ideas but I do need to be cognizant of other people's smart ideas so I can dovetail them into my plan. I photograph anything that interests me. I take lots of pictures. In fact, to effectively chronicle something that appeals to me, I not only photograph the idea but I also photograph a location sign and a magazine or newspaper showing the date. Then it's easy to remember where and when it was.

Let me give you an example. On one occasion I was driving on the freeway in France and pulled into a rest stop where there was a McDonalds. Inside the fast-food emporium they had several flat-screen TVs showing all of the food and drink options. You could make your selection and swipe your credit card to pay. It was so simple and effective; so beautifully done. I had to photograph it. I didn't know what I'd do with that particular idea—but I always capture something that is different and makes business sense. And I keep it on file.

That's one of the perks of international travel. You can discover what brilliant people are doing in many different countries and then bring those ideas home to incorporate into your own businesses or share with friends who have similar kinds of businesses.

Research

Let's continue with the same theme. Research is a critical component of any endeavor. Do your homework before taking the plunge. Study why good businesses succeed and why bad businesses fail. Here's my S.O.P. (standard operating procedure) using the restaurant business as an example. (The restaurant business, by the way, is probably one of the toughest businesses in the world).

Go into the best restaurants that you know. Take a paper and pencil with you (or just use your smartphone!) and write down everything you like about what they do—and what you don't like. Follow this procedure at different restaurants and you'll come up with a play book for running a successful restaurant operation.

So what aspects of the restaurant do you want to analyze? Here are some questions you should pose:

How's the décor? How's the ambience? Was I greeted cordially the moment I walked through the door? Was the staff dressed professionally? Was I seated promptly? If I couldn't be seated immediately was there somewhere to sit comfortably while I waited? Maybe they even provided a complimentary glass of wine? After I was seated, was the table clean? Was the silverware set properly? Was the waiter friendly and knowledgeable? Did the food smell good? Was it well presented? Was it warm? Did it taste good? Was the bathroom clean? All in all, was it a positive experience? Did the staff seem genuinely pleased to see me?

People go to places that they like; people go to places that like them.

There are dozens of things that contribute to the making of a successful business. So whatever business you want to start make sure you go into similar businesses first. Analyze what they're doing well and what they're doing wrong. Copy what they're doing well and avoid what they're doing wrong. And that brings me to another point:

You Don't Have To Be First

You don't have to be the pioneer. You don't have to come up with an innovative breakthrough concept that's never been done before. There's an old saying about pioneers being the people who end up with arrows in their backs. What you can do is spot something that's a proven success and leverage off of it as I mentioned in Chapter 2 discussing how I followed in my brother's footsteps opening a smog shop. Build that better mousetrap. If you can't improve something—don't.

Know Your Strengths and Weaknesses

I know a lot of people with big egos who have a hard time admitting that they're not good at something. But if you're going to develop a giant business enterprise you have to develop a team of people around you. This may not be breaking news, but you have to hire the best and the brightest. You have to hire people who are smarter than you in some aspects of the business.

It's remarkable to me that there are business leaders whose egos get in the way and they don't recruit the best because they're afraid of losing the limelight. You see this in middle management in a lot of companies. Don't be one of those people. Surround yourself with winners. If you're not good at something or don't like doing something hire someone who is. Find the right balance. If you want to scale, if you want to get big, you can't do it all. You've got to build a team.

One of my most important maxims which I constantly impress upon people: Make one of your strengths, knowing your weaknesses. I live by that. I've surrounded myself with people who can all do something better than I can.

After all, it doesn't make sense to spend your time doing the tasks at which you're weak. I am not an attorney, an accountant, a tax preparer, a computer programmer, for instance. I'm not a lot of things. I am a successful deal-maker and entrepreneur. I've always been able to acknowledge aspects of business that I'm good at and those that I'm not. So, to reiterate: I know my strengths. I know my weaknesses. Discover yours.

For instance, one of my partners who bought half of our company years ago is an incredible guy in many different ways. But you know what he does best? He's the Number One motivator. He's the motivator-in-chief. He's such a positive person. He fills everyone with confidence and he inspires the entire executive team to aspire to ever-greater accomplishments. That's quite a talent.

So, as your business grows you need to surround yourself with experts in other fields and hire people who are smarter than you in other ways. You build a team of trusted professionals. Get recommendations from people you trust; check references; interview diligently.

I use professional freelancers in specific fields of expertise. The website Upwork.com is one good resource.

Embrace Failure

Most of my businesses have been successful. Some have been great successes. But in order to become a success it's almost a requirement to have your share of failures. The key is being able to pick yourself up and go for it again. Identify what went wrong and learn from it. If a project is not working out, know when to call it quits. Accept that it was a mistake. Embrace the failure. It's a stepping stone towards success. Take it as part of your overall education and find something new to utilize your talents. Winners don't give up; winners bet on themselves. Winners aren't whiners. Winners don't think someone else is going to give them something for nothing. Winners go out and make it happen.

Test. Test. Test.

Before you spend a fortune launching a new business you should test to see if your concept is going to work in the real world. I've found that direct response advertising is an effective way to immediately get answers and know whether or not there is a demand for your product or service.

I once ran a TV infomercial and it completely failed to get the phones to ring. People just didn't want what the product that I was offering so I didn't waste any time. I acknowledged that it hadn't worked and I shut that deal down within a month. If something doesn't have that sweet taste of success, you move along.

Exceed Expectations

When you deliver more than you promised…when you deliver more than what was expected…you're going to develop a great reputation. Your customers or clients will keep coming back for more. And you'll have a thriving business. People will recognize that you're a person who gets things done; that you're a person they can count on.

If you own a restaurant, for example, you want to give better quality food at a better price than people expect. If you own a plumbing company you need to make sure your people show up on time, and provide the promised repairs at the agreed price. If you're a real estate sales person you need to go out of your way to take care of the home buyer or seller—and at every stage of the process. You want everyone to remember that they had a supremely positive experience.

If something goes wrong—you make amends. But do it smart and do it affordably. Back to the restaurant as an example: If someone is unhappy with their meal you're better off giving them a free dessert or a free cocktail rather than knocking the cost of the meal off their bill. You're giving them something with a high perceived value that doesn't cost you so much.

Don't worry about the five percent of customers who might try to take advantage of you. Always bear in mind the 95 percent of good people and how you should serve them.

Best in Breed

I've always felt that the right business model is to charge a fair price—or maybe even a higher price—but to do substantially the best work in the marketplace. Most people are more upset about getting a lousy quality product or service than they are about paying a little bit more.

If you do great work and people don't have to bug you to come back and correct something you will find people beating a path to your door. When you do more than you've agreed, when you surpass the terms of a contract, it's a simple law of nature that the beneficiary will tell everyone they know, and your business will grow. Let me give you some examples.

I've been in business for over 35 years. When I find someone who gives me no B.S., who treats me fairly and is honest, and tells me the truth when something doesn't really need to be repaired…they've got my business for life. There are numerous contractors—building, roofing, painting; whatever—that have got jobs from me time and time again without me getting other bids because they have proven themselves to me. Perhaps I could save money going elsewhere, but it saves me time—and my time is valuable. It saves me stress—and who wants stress? I continue to do business with them because of time, energy and effort. And their businesses continue to grow. Maybe they're not the cheapest, but they're honest and they do it right the first time.

You have to do the same when you're starting a business. Be honest with yourself. Constantly ask yourself: Is the quality of my work really the best? Am I charging fair prices? Do I deliver on schedule? And please don't fool yourself. A lot of people do fool themselves. Take a look in the mirror and honestly answer these three questions. If you think you're pulling a fast one, you're not. Most people are too nice to call your bluff and tell you upfront what they really think. But you can be sure that they won't hire you again. My partner and I have always believed in delivering more than we promise—it's one of the keys to our success.

Don't Be Greedy

Remember the famous line from the movie Wall Street, uttered by the Gordon Gekko character played by Michael Douglas? The one about greed being good? The full quote actually was: "The point is ladies and gentlemen that greed, for lack of a better word, is good." Well, I don't agree with that.

In business make it a win-win situation. You don't have to be the aggressive victor with every deal. Leave some money on the table. Your reputation will precede you and people will want to do business with you. I can't tell you how many times people have done business with my partner and me because, quite frankly, they enjoy it. They know we're not greedy and we want the deal to be beneficial for all of the parties involved. There's just no need for greed.

And, as I've said before and will say again: it's not all about the money. You need balance in your life. Success encompasses health, happiness and family. So, this chapter has given you some starting points. But there are a whole lot more as we'll discover in the next chapter.

Chapter 7. Make It Happen 2

We've only just begun! You're building your business…
but there's a long way to go before you can become
triumphant. There are many obstacles and pitfalls in the
way. So let's look at some of the issues that crop us as you
get out there and make it happen.

Ego vs. Ego

There's nothing wrong with having a healthy ego. Ego is
what has driven mankind to the pinnacle of success; to
develop mind-boggling inventions; build global businesses.
On the other hand, ego has driven mankind to be
belligerent and start wars. Ego can be destructive as well as
constructive.

But let me tell you about my experiences with people who
have giant egos. I like to say, "If a guy has a big ego and
he's going to do business with me, when he's done, he'll
have a bigger ego and I'll have a bigger checkbook."
Flatter the ego and you'll get what you want.

Negotiating with someone who has a huge ego is usually
fairly easy because large egos get you nowhere. Large egos
build animosity and most people don't like to be around
someone whose large ego is constantly on display. Try not
to have that kind of ego; instead be gracious, be nice, and
be kind. Walk into a room of powerful people with your
giant ego and you won't be well-liked and people won't
want to do business with you. Or, if they do business with
you, they'll pander to your ego, let you think you've out-
winked everybody and that you're the smartest guy in the
room, while, in fact, they're outsmarting you.

Do you think you might be a braggart? Do you think you might come on too strong? If the thought crosses your mind the chances are that you're right. But ask your friends for an honest opinion. Even people with unhealthy egos have friends.

Don't Burn Bridges

Let's say you've had a bad experience. Someone has let you down—or cheated you in a deal. You know it and they know it. But, it's done. There's no point in shooting off your mouth or shooting off an angry mean-spirited email telling him what an asshole he is. You never know what's going to happen in the future. You just never know when that individual is going to turn up with an attractive proposition. If that happens you're forewarned. You know the character of the person with whom you're dealing.

I've definitely had people who have screwed me come back a year or two later with information or a lead that led to a lucrative money-making proposition. I may have mentally written this individual off and decided I certainly wouldn't ever approach them again. I didn't bother to tell them how unfair I thought they had been. I buried my ego and let it go. I believe in the old adage, "If you can't say something nice, don't say anything at all." Would I ever call that person again? No? Would I take their call? Probably not. Would I listen to a message or read their email? Yes, I'll take a look. Of course, I'm going to be 100 percent cautious. I'll pay them a finder's fee but I'm not going to have them in the middle of the deal. However, I'm also not going to burn the bridges.

Dress For Success

Remember the book Dress for Success? I think it got it right. A businessperson should always look good. When you look good, you feel good. When you feel good you will have a positive mental attitude. When you have a positive mental attitude success comes your way. People like to deal with you. They don't want to deal with people who are negative.

There's no doubt in my mind that a well-dressed person looks more honest and professional. When I'm hiring someone first impressions do count…and a major first impression is how well someone looks. I definitely pay attention to how well-kempt the person is. And not just their clothing or grooming. What about their car? It doesn't matter what kind of car. It doesn't have to be a big, fancy car, but I want to see that the car is clean and well maintained.

How should you dress? Times have changed and what was the cultural norm 20 years ago is vastly different today. And every situation is different. What you're going to wear as a plumber is different to what you'll wear as a computer programmer or a realtor. The bottom line is that whatever your occupation, the person who looks more professional will make people feel more secure.

Don't Just Sit There—Speak Up

Mention public speaking and most people shudder. The fear of having to speak in public is the number one fear in America—followed by death! I have to admit that even after 30 years of making presentations in public, I don't go out of my way to be a public speaker. But if it's an important forum where I need to get my message across, I get on and do it. I'm a relatively shy person at heart but I have forced myself to be a good public speaker because in order to be a successful leader or entrepreneur, and to grow in your industry, it goes with the territory.

There's a group that can help called Toastmasters. It's basically free and I urge you to check it out. Go online to Toastmasters.org and find a meeting near you. Attend just one meeting and you will see how this organization can introduce you to the skills of public speaking. Please make a commitment to do this. When you speak in public, when you make public appearances, your credibility builds. The more you do it, the more capable you will become. You will be perceived as an expert in your field—and you will attract business.

I actually credit Toastmasters with giving me the ability and confidence to speak in front of large crowds.

On one occasion there was an audience of 7,500 people. It was an event being staged by a large seminar organization at the Javits Center in New York. Other speakers included Donald Trump and Tony Robbins. If it hadn't been for my training and experience I would have been scared to death. Nevertheless, I was still somewhat nervous when I hit the stage and I was out there by myself in front of all those people. So yes, it was a little overwhelming. But I sold about $250,000 of land subdivisions in about four minutes flat. So it was worth it!

The ability to stand up and speak in public helps in other situations, too; for instance, whenever toasts have to be given at a wedding or other celebration or when a eulogy is required at a funeral. But it's definitely a skill that needs to be cultivated to become an accomplished leader.

Don't Talk Too Much

I've just finished telling you how to give a good talk and now I'm encouraging you not to talk?! What's up with that? Here's what I mean. You've no doubt heard the expression, "Loose lips sink ships."

It originated on propaganda posters in the states during World War II. The goal was to alert servicemen and others to the dangers of careless talk concerning secure information that might be of use to the enemy— specifically, in this case, to refrain from speaking of ship movements.

The same rule applies in business. When you have a good thing going don't be a big-mouth and blabber about it to the world. That's only going to be to your detriment. When you've got a great idea share it on a 'need to know' basis. I appreciate it can be hard to keep quiet when you're excited about the potential of a pet project, but discussing it freely is a fool's game. If you have something truly proprietary make sure people sign a Non-Disclosure Agreement (NDA) before you share it with them.

Winning Friends

My favorite all-time book that's an absolute must-read for anyone seeking business success is Dale Carnegie's How to Win Friends and Influence People. It was an immediate success when it was first published in 1937 and its advice is just as sound now more than three quarters of a century and 15 million copies later.

Dale Carnegie had an understanding of human nature that will never be outdated. He felt that 15 percent of financial and business success could be attributed to professional knowledge and 85 percent to "the ability to express ideas, to assume leadership, and to arouse enthusiasm among people."

Read Carnegie's book and you will understand how to deal with people in such a cool and kind manner that they will naturally be attracted to you. Not only will your business relationships become better and you will become more successful but your personal relationships will also improve.

If you want to be successful you need to read his book— at least twice. You need to understand its teachings and put them into practice. I give this book away all the time to people who have the desire to improve their position in life. It's inexpensive and pays for itself countless times over. I looked it up on Amazon the other day and it was rated number 37 in current bestsellers. That's amazing after 75 years.

Getting Organized

You're not going to get anywhere if you're disorganized. You've got to keep on top of your day-to-day activities and how they fit into your long-term business strategy. One of the simplest ways of all is keeping a 'to-do' list. I always put the most important projects first and I re-do the list every day depending on how priorities have changed.

Today, my goal is to only touch a document or piece of correspondence once. I read it, make my decision, put a sticky note on the top with that decision and move along. You can also, of course, go paperless. There are some great software products on the market which enable you to scan receipts and business cards and all kinds of documents and catalog them into a paperless environment.

Mentors

Find as many good mentors as you can! I've been lucky to have had many as I discussed earlier in the book.

Over the years I've I learned much more by talking with successful business people than I have from talking with professionals like my lawyers and accountants. These are often great professionals within their sphere of knowledge. They're great for giving me legal advice and accounting advice, but typically they're conservative by nature. They don't necessarily have the business acumen. What you need from the mentoring standpoint is someone who is a peak-performing entrepreneur in your industry, someone who has had the hands-on experience.

Outside of family I've been lucky to have four or five extremely accomplished mentors in my life who became good friends, and who I could call on for advice at any time. Of course, it's a two-way street. Once you become successful and established and have built your own credentials the same guys know that they can call on you for a favor. I always reciprocate. I want to become indispensable to them, so they are always happy to help with advice and give me some mental clarity on issues. Being able to call someone who has already walked down a path, being able to call someone who has lived your problems, is huge. They can give you advice that you just can't acquire elsewhere without making a mistake to learn it. As we've discussed earlier, one of the keys to being successful is to learn from other people's mistakes.

How do you find a mentor?

You need to emulate people that you respect and want to be like. And, most importantly, let them know that! Seek out the leaders in your chosen industry. Find out where the big boys play. Where do they hang out? What do they do for fun? What organizations and clubs do they belong to? Figure out how to get in front of them. Reach out to them. When you manage that—be humble. Listen. Listen hard. Ask good questions. You may well find that they know about deals that are too small for them, but are big for you, and they're happy to refer them to you since they now know you and know your abilities.

Whatever you do, don't waste their time. When you say you're going to do something, do it. One of the reasons I have had such good relationships with my mentors is that they know that I act on the solid advice they give me. The other thing you have to do as a good mentee is report back on your progress and let your mentor share in the mental glory of your achievement. And, of course, when they need help you need to be there for them. That's how you build long-term mentor-mentee relationships that are very satisfying for all parties concerned.

Now that I've become a mentor myself it's very rewarding to see someone else succeed based on my input —even more so when they share news of their triumphs with me. What is frustrating, though, is when you mentor someone and they never take action. Most mentors are not going to want to hang out for too long with people who don't take action.

I'm in my fifties now. If someone contacts me and asks a question I'm happy to give my advice, especially because I don't worry about competition any more. I like to see young people succeed like I succeeded.

I've become good friends with all of my mentors because they know that I care about them. I really care about them. I care about their well-being. I care about their health. I care about any of the trials and tribulations of life that they endure. If you want someone to care about you, you have to care about them. One excellent example: I have a 94-year-old buddy who is the smartest real estate guy I know. He still remembers more than I do and I still call him for advice.

Don't Be a Quitter

Never give up. One of the most important elements of success is sticking to your guns when you have a great idea and not stopping until it's accomplished. I became successful because I refused to not become successful. I wouldn't take no for an answer. Yes, like almost every successful entrepreneur I have had my share of failures, but I always had a vision and worked like heck to get there.

If it was a particularly big goal I would always start with the end in sight and work backwards from it, asking myself what I needed to do yearly, monthly, weekly, daily and then hourly to achieve it. My first land auction was a one year project and I worked on it day and night until it happened. I made a commitment and I took it seriously. In the meantime you might have to forego some of the fun things in life, but those are the sacrifices that have to be made.

Make Yourself Lucky

How do you make yourself lucky? You make yourself lucky by working hard, getting out in front of enough people, telling them what you're doing, and by making noise. I made myself lucky selling real estate by sending out tons of letters and enough people who got them would say, "Oh my gosh. I was just thinking of selling that property. This is an omen."

You can make good luck or you can make bad luck. If you treat people right, you probably generate good luck. If you have bad ethics, you will create bad luck. I firmly believe that what goes around comes around. Karma, if you want to call it that.

You make yourself lucky by doing thorough research so that when the right opportunity arrives you're ready to pounce on it. I've been in commercial real estate for a long time. I can now look at a deal and tell you within minutes if it's a good deal.

You make yourself lucky by taking calculated risks because you've educated yourself first. You know the cost of raw commodities. You know the cost of labor. You have real numbers on which you can make a decision.

You make yourself lucky by being pro-active. In my younger days we used to drive around looking at buildings and then take the initiative and approach people asking if they wanted to sell. There were times when we were able to buy properties even before they came on the market. You never know when you're going to find someone wealthy who has an asset they want to get rid of and you might get it at a wonderful price because the timing was right.

You make yourself lucky by stretching beyond your comfort zone. Period. In whatever you do.

You make yourself lucky by being in the right place at the right time and taking action.

You make yourself lucky by getting out there and asking. You create opportunities. And it doesn't necessarily have to cost you anything. You can place blind ads on Craigslist, for instance, or in your local newspaper getting exposure and making your needs known.

You have to be visible.

This might begin to sound a bit like marketing yourself—and it is. Which leads us onto a chapter which offers some specific—and basic—marketing tips based on my career.

Chapter 8. Marketing 101

I've tried and tested numerous ways of marketing and I've also carefully studied and analyzed what others have done—especially the competition. Let me share some key strategies with you that you should consider whatever your business might be.

Target Marketing

First of all, you have to establish your target market. Who is your universe of buyers? Is it a big universe? Are you selling a car and you know that almost every adult in the country wants to own a car? Are you selling a television and you know that every household will have one or two or three or sometimes even more televisions? If that's the case you'll be able to use a broadly-based advertising strategy— national TV and radio, for instance, because you want to reach a wide swathe of consumers. The same applies to selling Coke or Budweiser. It's a shotgun approach.

On the other hand if you are selling a very specific type of microchip and you know that only 100 manufacturers in the world need it then your advertising strategy, of necessity, must be much finely focused. In this case you'd contact the companies directly with emails, letters, phone calls and knocking on their door. Spending money on a big national advertising campaign would be nonsense. It's a rifle approach.

Let's look at Auction.com as an example of a company where both approaches have to be deployed.

Selling homes is a big market. More than five million are sold every year in the states. There's high demand for a high ticket item. Homes are being sold all over the country so a broadly-based advertising strategy promoting the Auction.com platform is effective—TV, radio, newspapers, and the Internet. The more people that see us and the more aware they become of Auction.com, the better.

But we also have a commercial division. And that's a much narrower market. So in this instance we target people who are known buyers of commercial properties or have a need for the particular kind of building that's available. We might narrow it even further to people who already own similar property within a five mile radius. The more you can fine tune your promotional activities the more efficient your advertising budget will become.

Selling hamburgers is another interesting case study. If I'm McDonalds my advertising is going to be on a larger, broader scale, of course, than if I own a mom and pop corner stand. If I'm McDonalds I can run national TV advertising and know that I'm reaching my demographic because I have locations everywhere. But if I'm the owner of Rob's hamburger shack in Anaheim, California and that's my one and only location I need to focus on getting my message out to my local community as inexpensively as possible. I'm probably hoping to just reach folks within the radius of a few miles. The local newspaper is an obvious choice, or any of the free sheets. Or there might be a really local radio station, that's worth a test. A bigger regional newspaper is almost certainly going to cost too much and reach people who won't want to drive 20 miles to check out the quality of your burgers. Everything has to be tested—no matter how big or small a "campaign."

Shotgun or rifle? It shouldn't be hard to decide!

Relationship Marketing

Let's never forget that people do business, more often than not, with people they like. And people who like them and/or are like them. People do business with people who look like them and dress like them. They do business with people who have friends in common, who went to the same school, or belong to the same church, the same club, or the same fraternity.

People do business with people who show sincere gratitude and care about them. The more you can put yourself in the shoes of your client, the greater the likelihood you will develop an ongoing relationship. But make sure you become a worthy friend. The kind of individual that someone knows that they can count on for help even after the deal is done. You'll have a more satisfying life as a result.

Reaching out on a continuing basis shows that you remember and you care. Birthday cards. Holiday cards. Any kind of card or small thoughtful gift builds your infrastructure to success. To this day my partner and I send out hundreds of holiday gifts to good business friends as a means of staying in touch and showing that we care. I'm delighted and proud to say that I've had numerous clients who have turned into really good friends.

Be sure to always know with whom you're dealing. Can you remember the names of your clients? Their wives' names? Their kids' names? That's all part of relationship marketing. Politicians are particularly adept at being able to acknowledge people they meet by name. People love it when that happens.

Business Reciprocation

If someone does a favor for you its human nature to want to repay it. People nearly always want to return the compliment. Even in business situations where you're shown common hospitality by being offered something to eat or drink you feel a certain sense of obligation. I think back to the days when I owned my stereo stores and wonder if I could have increased sales even more if I'd given everyone a soda or a small gift as they walked in the door—because people like to feel they have been treated well. And then they feel the need to reciprocate.

When I was growing up one of my favorite restaurants in Anaheim, California was Mama Cozza's. It's no accident that they've been in business for almost 50 years. As soon as you sat down they'd deliver a really nice little relish tray to the table. At the end of the meal they'd give you a shot of Anisette. They treated everybody like a friend. I truly believe that—apart from the good food—one of their reasons for success was the little extras they provided. It gave you a warm feeling, made you feel important, and made you want to return.

So, think about it. What can you do to make your clients feel comfortable and want to reciprocate?

Testimonials

Early on when we got started building REDC, the precursor to Auction.com, we quickly learned that if we did a good job for someone and they wrote us a letter of recommendation it had much more impact in our next direct mail pitches to potential clients.

The letter would say something like:

Dear Rob,

I told you that if you did a great job for me I would send you this letter so you could use my name with potential clients.

Well, you guys did a great job. You sold all of my houses and I want to personally thank you for everything you did. It gives me great pride to recommend you to all of my colleagues in the building industry that might need an auction.

Yours,

_____

This kind of letter was extremely valuable and helped our business grow. In brochures or any kind of correspondence it is so much better to have a testimonial from someone else rather than you beating your own chest. It's perfect to have someone else brag about you, but you don't want to brag about yourself.

If you can get a celebrity or someone of high standing in the community, that's even better. I saw the incredible power of celebrity testimonials when we produced an infomercial for the land auction business. Initially we used a no-name broadcaster who did a really good job. But when we switched to a big name we got three times the number of phone calls. So celebrities can really pay for themselves.

Think of it this way: A testimonial is an endorsement for either the business or you as a good person. Obviously the bigger the name, the better. If it's someone like a General, for instance, it's really meaningful because this individual is staking his reputation on you.

When you get great testimonials use them extensively. Use them whenever and wherever you can. On the internet.

Radio. TV. Print. Everywhere. And if it is a visual medium, a photograph of the individual is even more powerful.

Vanity Phone Numbers

What's a vanity phone number? You're a taxi service and you have a number that spells out 1-800-CALL-TAXI. You have a plumbing service and your number is 1-800-PLUMBER. The learn-to-read program Hooked on Phonics had a great number: 1-800-ABC-DEFG. And, of course, there's 1-800-FLOWERS.

Vanity numbers work because they are memorable. They work particularly well, for instance, when people are driving by a billboard or listening to an ad on the radio and cannot write down the number.

Of course, getting a good sequence of numbers not associated with a specific word works just as well if not better: 1-800-777-7777 as an example. As time goes on, though, it's getting harder to acquire such numbers. They can be worth thousands. The best numbers can sell for anywhere between $25,000 and $50,000. To find appropriate vanity numbers just do a Google search for "vanity phone brokers."

Keeping Track

Generating inquiries and orders is nothing but the first step in building a business. You need to build your database. You need to keep track of specifically what advertising medium generated business and how much it cost you. A $1,000 TV commercial on Station XYZ that generated 100 leads is obviously more cost-effective than a $500 TV commercial on Station MNO that generated 20 leads. In the first instance, your Cost Per Lead (CPL) is $10.00; in the second instance it's $25.00. But do you know that?

When you're a small business and running only a handful of campaigns it's easy to put together a spreadsheet and keep track. When you're bigger you can acquire more sophisticated programming. Always code your advertising so you can assign it to the correct source. Put letters/numbers on a direct mail coupon. Or, with internet advertising, for instance, have customers enter a special word to get their discount.

And do those leads turn into customers? Do those customers turn into repeat customers? What do you know about those customers? Why didn't they make a purchase? What specifically do they need to know the next time you call them? When are you going to call them? You need to enter all of this information (and more) into a spreadsheet and, when affordable, pay for good Customer Relations Management (CRM) software such as Salesforce.com.

When you're inter-acting with a customer you should always make a point of asking, "How did you hear about us?" You need to know which advertising medium to credit for the business. If you're lucky maybe it came word-of-mouth because your guys provided superb service!

Keep refining your ways of keeping track. It's imperative to know who your customers are and where they came from. An incremental increase of one or two percent can add up to greater profitability.

Loss Leader

If you remember my earlier story about the pen watch drawing huge crowds to our stereo shop you know I'm a big believer in loss leaders.

It's a marketing technique that works in all kinds of businesses.

Take auto dealerships, for example. You'll find a car advertised at a remarkably low price in the Friday or Saturday newspapers. Typically, it will be below dealer cost. But they'll only have one at that price and to get it you'll probably have to be first in line at 5 or 6 a.m. It's probably going to be a color that most people don't like and it will be devoid of any special features. That's all because they're going to do their darndest to sell you a different (and more expensive) model once they've got you in the door.

They lose money on the loss leader. It's unethical and illegal if they don't have that loss leader to sell you when the ad breaks, even if it's just one car. It's bait and switch if they don't have it. But, regardless, the reality is that they're going to go all-out to upsell you to a sexier model loaded with extras. It's the same with companies offering to give your car an oil change at a ridiculously low price. Yes, they are duty-bound to honor that offer, but they'll definitely try to get you to buy other services. And that's absolutely fine as long as it's done in an honest and ethical way.

Recommended Reading

A good resource is Harvey Mackay's "Swim with the Sharks without Being Eaten Alive."

So, this chapter has been a simple introduction to basic marketing techniques that work. But the biggest earth-shaking development in recent memory is the development of the Internet and the whole new world of marketing opportunities it has introduced. The next chapter is devoted to that medium.

Chapter 9. Internet Marketing 101

We live in a digital word, a fast-paced, ever-changing digital world. Just consider the monumental disruption there has been as a result of the introduction of the Internet to the public in the early 1990s.

Change is going to becoming increasingly dramatic. The publication Business Insider estimates, for example, that the number of devices connected to the Internet of Things is going to increase by a factor of 10 within five years. By 2019, the number will be almost 24 billion—way up from the 2014 number of 2.5 billion.

And according to Statista.com, U.S. retail e-commerce sales in 2012 amounted to $225.5 billion dollars and are projected to grow to $434.2 billion in 2017.

Look at what has already been impacted.

Think about the travel business. How many people go to a travel agent any more? It's just so convenient to search online for flights and hotels and vacation deals—and be spoiled by the profusion of choices.

Bookstores—they're disappearing. The goliath that is Amazon dominates. More and more people are also choosing to use e-readers like Kindle rather than carry hardcover books and paperbacks around.

Music. Once upon a time there were cassettes. They got wiped out by CDs. Now CDs are disappearing because most people, especially the younger generations, have turned to MP3 players and digital music downloads. Instant access!

Newspapers. Do you remember when people got their news from a daily newspaper that arrived on their doorstep? That's one of the jobs I had as a kid. I had a paper route delivering those newspapers early every morning. Today we get constant news updates on our laptops and smartphones.

For those people who adapt and move with the times, however, the Internet is a mind-boggling opportunity. And anyone can participate—anyone. It really levels the playing field.

I obviously speak from personal experience. Auction.com is the nation's leading online real estate marketplace and in September, 2014 I was honored to be named Internet Person of the Year by the Internet Marketing Association. I was particularly delighted and humbled to join previous honorees such as Mark Zuckerberg of Facebook; Tony Hsieh, CEO of Zappos; and Justin Choi, founder of Nativo. So, let's explore some of the basics.

Website

The first, most essential thing that any business needs is a website—in effect an electronic brochure for your business. If that's something that is outside of your realm of knowledge and expertise, don't worry. Use the Internet to help. Simply do a Google search for the kind of business or service that you plan to start or improve. There will probably be hundreds of sites. Take the time to review them and save the links and/or print hard copies of the ones you like so that you can share them with your web designer of choice.

Domain Names

A natural progression from easy-to-remember vanity phone numbers that we discussed in the last chapter was the creation of domain names. A friend told me about them in

1994 when the Internet was first lifting off, it immediately hit me that obtaining some really cool domain names would be a good investment. Remember—this was back in 1994. The rules at the time dictated that you could only acquire one domain name per business entity. They cost about $70.00 each. We didn't really know what would be big but we knew for sure that billions of people were interested in football and basketball so I registered Football.com and Basketball.com, and also Trivia.com and Netad.com.

I still own them today and they're worth a lot of money. In my estimation each domain that cost $70.00 is now worth at least $1 million. That's a pretty good investment. (Remember, we paid nearly $1.8 million to acquire the Auction.com domain name so we fully appreciate the value of perfect domain names). In fact I was offered several million dollars for the domain Football.com but I declined because I didn't really approve of the business that wanted to acquire it—an offshore gambling pirate.

Instead, we've gone ahead and done our own thing and we are building Football.com to become the largest site of its kind on the web. I will write more about Football.com and my other domains at the end of this chapter.

Design: Now go to a website like Upwork.com where you can find hundreds of independent freelance web developers (or find someone locally) and get them to quote on producing a site for you. Show them what you like and what you don't like and cover all the bases of what you need to include. On Upwork I recommend that you work with a company or individual that has high satisfaction ratings from previous clients. Don't just take the first company with whom you have a conversation. You will be amazed at the difference in the bids if you shop around. Often you can find someone who is really talented who for a variety of personal reasons is willing to do a highly professional job at a very reasonable price.

Another alternative is to use a website template that has been designed by someone with exceptional talent. Just change the photos and verbiage to fit your project. That's what I've done for a charity with which I'm involved. The overall flow of the site is fabulous and would have cost thousands of dollars if it had been designed from scratch specifically for our purpose.

Content: A great design is one thing, but a winning website needs content that's worth reading and that will appeal to your target audience. Again, you can hire a professional writer who specializes in your industry and have him put together some new unique content that the search engine will rate highly and will help propel your site to the top of the search engine lists. Keep that content updated because the search engines constantly crawl through sites to check for fresh information or perspective. Or get your site mentioned on other sites. These are important strategies to get what we call organic search hits (the best kind of traffic). If done correctly you'll have fresh and interesting content that the search engine will like (through their sophisticated algorithm) and you'll get a ton of traffic to your site.

Search Engine Optimization: The next step is the deployment of Search Engine Optimization (SEO). Hire a specialist or learn how to do it yourself. It's a way of using certain words to describe your product and service so that your site gets picked up by the search engines. There's a complicated, and very interesting formula why the search engines like some sites and not others—and it's well worth discovering. You can also find freelancers to write SEO blogs very affordably.

   Contact: Make sure that a visitor to your site has multiple options for contacting you—a contact form, email address, toll free phone number and maybe even a live online chat. Make sure there are no roadblocks! If they're interested you can't afford to lose them at this stage.

   Marketing: Congratulations. By building a search engine friendly website in the first place you've already started your online marketing. The best form of traffic is the free traffic or organic traffic that comes to your site because they saw you had written a great article. In the best of all worlds that would be all the marketing we needed to do. Unfortunately, there's much more to it than that! Next you have to consider Search Engine Marketing (SEM).

   Search Engine Marketing

   You've probably noticed that when you do a Google search there are links at the top and side of the page that have a little white on orange icon that says Ad or Ads. That's because companies are paying for what Google calls AdWords—key words that are direct hits to your type of business (FYI you pick the words). The interesting thing is that Google basically holds an auction to see who will pay the most for premium listings (those at the top of the page). For obscure key words (and smaller less profitable business groups) key words can cost a few cents. But in high-priced businesses—plastic surgery or personal injury attorneys, for example—the cost can be $30 to $40, or more, per click. The way it works is pretty simple: you have basically made a deal with the search engine which says I will pay you x amount every time someone clicks on the link that brings them to my website.

Obviously, if you're selling a really expensive item or a service where your profit margin is high you can afford to pay a higher amount per click as long as those clicks convert to deals or contracts. Keep in mind that you must always track all of your advertising so you know which one is most cost effective.

So, as a simple example if you're a bridge builder and each contract is worth millions of dollars there will be very few people looking for bridge builders. But they are extremely valuable contacts and it is important for you to get the opportunity to talk with them. In this case it's probably worth paying hundreds of dollars for that click. On the other hand, if you're a barber just down the street you probably want to pay less than a dollar per click to reach local people looking for a haircut.

Also, whenever you're paying for any kind of advertising, it is not necessarily the profit you make on the first deal but the profit you will make over the lifetime of that client that is vital to consider. It's different for each business. For example, if that barber knows that his average customer comes back 10 times it would be reasonable to pay more for the initial click.

Banner Ads: There are other advertising strategies. One of the easiest is to produce a banner ad (those small ads usually 1 inch by 6 inch that you see on most websites). Pay for them to appear on websites that are appropriate for your service. For example, if you have an auto repair shop it would be a good idea to run your ad on websites for auto enthusiasts. If your market is brides-to-be you definitely want to run your banners on wedding websites. Take some time to sit and think what would work best for you.

Monitor Results: The key is to get a simple system that tracks where an ad runs, how many clicks it gets and how many of those clicks convert to deals (see Google Analytics). Icannot emphasize enough: the better you can track your advertising the more you can figure out where to spend your advertising budget most effectively. Don't ever prejudge and think you know the answer. Let the results speak for themselves through the statistics and TEST TEST TEST. Rotate five different ads and find the winner. Then put the winner up against five more ads and keep testing before you roll out a big campaign. You don't need to be an expert. You can find someone on Upwork (and elsewhere) to set it up for you.

Retargeting: Another very cool marketing technique is called search retargeting. In this approach sophisticated platforms will look at the searches your potential clients have made in the past and make sure you're serving up ads relevant to what they're looking for. So, for example, if you search "buy house in Anaheim Calif" we would know to show you ads that specifically showed you houses in that area. Very powerful.

Email marketing: Now let's talk about email marketing. The interesting thing about email marketing is it's probably the most cost effective advertising I have ever used. The smart thing to do is build an email database via your website and any other method of communication that you have with potential clients. Email this list with interesting information: news updates, lessons, special offers, and special events, for instance. There are some excellent systems to help you manage this list. Google the phrase "email marketing systems" and review all of the platforms. I cannot stress enough how important it is to keep in touch with your clients, to remind them of your presence and the great service or product you provide. When you get more experienced and sophisticated you can personalize your email so each recipient feels it was sent just to them. The salutation will be personalized and spelled correctly and it will be appreciated by the recipient. Make your clients feel important every step of the way.

Do whatever it takes to build that email list, even if you have to collect the email addresses on paper and enter them yourself. It could pay dividends. Analyze emails that come to you and study the techniques other marketers are using to get the responses they desire. Read books and learn. Remember that's how you make yourself lucky.

Facebook, etc.

You probably already have a Facebook page. Maybe Instagram and Pinterest, YouTube and Tumblr, too. It wouldn't be surprising if you're on Facebook because there are 1.44 billion monthly active users. And they spend an average of 21 minutes a day on Facebook. So these social media sites represent the new frontier of marketing, especially for the younger generations. I recommend you look for full-length books on the topic.

Final Note: I am not going into great detail on any of the Internet Marketing techniques because I'm not personally an expert in this field. I am, however, an expert at finding experts who can help fulfill my goals very quickly. I have just scratched the surface to make you aware of the opportunities that exist and must be pursued. But if you want to educate yourself you can find some excellent books on the subject on Amazon. And let me emphasize one final time that the essence of a great marketing campaign is the testing and tracking. When you find the winning formula then you roll it out big-time.

Football.com, etc.

Now let me give you a personal example—my development of Football.com. As I mentioned earlier I acquired the domain back in 1994 (along with other valuable names like Basketball.com, Trivia.com and Netad.com). I have not rushed to do anything with them because I have always believed that if something is worth doing, it's worth doing well. At the right time, with the right partners. But now Football.com is becoming a reality of staggering proportions.

Our goal (pun intended) is to change the way football is experienced on the planet—American Football and International Football (Soccer). Football.com is the "everything football" website. Anything and everything you could possibly want to know—or do—that's connected with football will be on this site.

It's the online resource for every player, every team and every league worldwide. In fact, however you are connected with the sport you will find a place, whether you're a player, trainer, referee, team owner, retailer, manufacturer, writer, blogger, photographer—or cheerleader.

Football.com will carry every statistic imaginable at every level of personal, amateur and professional games. It will carry results of games, league standings, and individual performance records. Our team of hundreds of top-notch writers will provide a host of reports and columns, constantly updated.

We start with giving little kids their own page where they can track their own sports metrics and we go on to help teams with their fundraising activities and identifying kids for recruiters. It will allow coaches to spend more time on the field and not in their office. It will enable the management of leagues to operate more efficiently and will facilitate all kinds of payment processing. It's a huge proposition. It's the most advanced sports management website that has ever been constructed and to make it happen we've invested several million dollars using a highly talented team of international developers.

I don't yet have a clear vision for Basketball.com and Trivia.com because I'm waiting to find the right partner. However, we already get a ton of traffic every day on those domains just because people type in those names. So the potential is there.

But that's business potential. And that's only part of life. Next, I'm going to address other values that together make a good life complete.

Chapter 10. Living Life Right

What do I mean by "Living Life Right?"

I mean always doing the right thing. Leading an honorable existence. Being decent. Not ripping people off. Taking care of your body and mind, of course. Becoming financially healthy! And getting the right kind of education.

Let's look first at taking care of your body.

I do believe in the old tenet, "The early bird gets the worm." I often go to bed at 10 and get up at 6 so I get my eight hours of sleep. I do my work-outs. I eat properly—lots of fruits and vegetables and good natural foods. I have a healthy discipline.

Get Healthy

Here's another old saying that happens to be true: If you don't have your health you don't have anything. If you're overweight, if you smoke, if you over-indulge in alcohol or other bad habits it's going to be all the harder to secure what I consider to be a well-rounded, happy and healthy business and family lifestyle.

If your path to business success is being hindered by drinking too much or doing drugs 12 step programs like Alcoholics Anonymous and Narcotics Anonymous can be a phenomenal help. In fact, some of the strongest people I know have made it happen after going through one of these programs. Perhaps that's because typical Type A personalities do everything to the extreme.

Quite frankly, following many of the 12-step guidelines—even if you don't have a problem—can make a major difference in your life. So—if you feel the need—get yourself a sponsor and embrace these programs. If you have a family member or friend who needs help, point them in the right direction. They really are righteous programs.

So, getting healthy means eating right and exercising. And getting rid of those bad habits. Are you willing to make a commitment? Let's explore the options.

Drinking

Personally, I think you can drink in moderation. A glass or two of wine, or the occasional beer or vodka won't hurt you. But there's nothing redeeming about drinking. Let's keep it to a mild roar—one or two a day at most. (I choose vodka because it's low in calories!).

Smoking

Quit! If you're smoking, stop right now. It really is that simple. It's the single worst thing you can do to your body. I know you've heard it a million times but that doesn't make it any less true. Do whatever it takes. Use a patch or medication. If you want to smoke, smoke. But you're going to die young, and that's not successful. I remember when I was in my teens a good friend who was probably in his forties (and the father of a girlfriend) told me how much he enjoyed smoking because it was fun. A few years later I heard he was dying of cancer! He had six children and it seemed such a waste of a life and devastating to such a large family. Everyone has their choices in life. If that's what you dig, if that's what you want…then do it, in the full knowledge that it's a fool's game. Your call. Even if it could mean last call.

Exercising

Start. Right now. If you're not already exercising you need to get out there and do something. Anything. Make a commitment to get up at a certain time in the morning and exercise. For me it's 6:00 A.M. at least three to four times a week. Surely, you could do a 30-minute walk, for starters, just three or four times a week? It will sharpen your mental prowess, too. Or maybe join a gym or try yoga? A body that's in shape has to be more sexually appealing. Wouldn't you want that?

Eating

Let's eat what the Almighty gave us—and by that I mean fresh fruits, fresh vegetables, and lots of fresh legumes. Figure out how you like to prepare them so you thoroughly enjoy eating them. But, sorry; not a lot of butter, and not a lot of fat. Choose heart healthy fats. Stop the fried foods. Stop the added sugar. Personally, I'm not a vegetarian but I think that's a great way of life if you can make that commitment.

Your body as well as your mind needs to be in optimal shape to get where we want it to go. And there are no shortcuts.

Financial

Let's turn from a healthy body to healthy financial planning.

The first $10,000 that you earn or save is going to be the hardest. Don't squander it. Savor it. Use it wisely.

I'm a firm believer in living within your means and saving…not just for a rainy day but as a way for having the financial resources to make an investment or seize a business opportunity when the time is right.

I'll give you a simple example. You're a journeyman plumber. You've worked for the same boss for years. He likes you and he's decided to retire. He'll give you all of his accounts and the equipment—basically just for the cost of the equipment. It's a wonderful opportunity. But you've lived beyond your means and you haven't saved a dime. You can't buy the business. You can't become your own boss. And if someone else takes over—maybe you won't even have a job. It could be any kind of business. You've been there a while. The owner likes you. He or she is willing to sell the business to you, but you've been spending beyond your means and you miss out big-time.

The same kind of thing can happen in any career. You could become a real expert. You could have real talent and a valuable, life-changing opportunity passes your way and you have to take a pass because you don't have the capital. Or maybe you're a coin collector and you have the chance to acquire a great coin at a ridiculously low price. But you have no financial reserve. Opportunity lost.

So let's discuss getting your financial act together from day one. Let's look at commonsense items where you can save money every day. Let's analyze our day-to-day lives and where all of the money goes. How we live our lives, what we eat, how we dress, where we live, what kind of car we drive, and so forth.

Frugality

Okay. I am now going to wear my Mr. Frugal hat. It has served me well.

What are you drinking right now? Do you have a soda sitting in front of you? How much did it cost? Perhaps you could have filled a water bottle with water from a fountain. It's fine to drink. It's healthier for you. And it costs nothing. By drinking sodas you're contributing to poor health and spending money on a worthless product. How many sodas a day do you consume? What does that cost per day? Not a fortune, right? But what does it cost over the course of a year?

What about cigarettes? Apart from being the biggest hazard to your health they're also one of the biggest hazards to your wallet. Have you noticed how much they've increased in cost over the years as taxes have skyrocketed in an effort to stop people indulging in this habit? Quit now and put that money in an interest-bearing account (not a piggy bank!).

Coffee? I enjoy going to Starbucks as much as the next person but we're talking here about saving money and you can always brew something at home (even if it isn't as good!). Forgoing a cup of coffee a day at a coffee shop could save you $1,000 a year! It all adds up. And remember, it's not just that $1,000. To make that money you would have to have earned double or one-and-a-half times as much because of the taxes you pay. Imagine what you could do with an extra $1,000 plus.

Cocktails? Wine? Beer? Your 'poison' of choice doesn't matter. Have a drink at home instead of at a fancy bar where you also have to pay a tip for the pleasure of someone pouring it for you. Reward yourself with the tip.

The same goes for food. Of course, I'm not saying that you should eat at home all the time (even if buying fresh food and cooking for yourself is healthier as well as cheaper). But you don't have to go to a crazily expensive

Michelin Guide restaurant; you can find somewhere more affordable with good food.

You don't have to get front row seats at a concert or game, either; you can find cheaper seats. Or watch it on TV. Taking your own bag of peanuts to a ballgame is also not the end of the world.

What's important is to put your money into purchasing a home and investments with a guaranteed rate of return and not squandering it on entertainment. And, yes, when I was younger and really watching my pennies I didn't have a problem cutting coupons and eating out where-ever I got a deal. And take note: if you go to the supermarket and apples are on sale—you buy apples. If you go to the store and nectarines are on sale—you buy nectarines. It's commonsense.

It's all about saving money and living below your means. So let's cut your overhead.

Let's take a look at the place where you live and the car that you drive. These are the two biggest expenditures virtually everyone incurs.

Where are you living? How are you living? Do you really need the big apartment and the high-end furniture? Who are you trying to impress?

Do you really need that flashy car with the huge monthly payments? Perhaps you could have found a good quality used car and paid cash? No payments. No debt. That's what I do. I typically buy cars that are a year or two old, with 10,000 to 20,000 miles on the clock. I pay cash, and I drive them for four or five years.

By the way, if you're in a personal relationship it's important that your other half is on the same page. Otherwise you've got real problems. If your significant other can't roll with it, you've probably got the wrong significant other.

All of these tips are one step at a time, one day at a time. Achieving success is no different to growing a forest…you plant one seed at a time. Nothing happens overnight. You can choose to be a show-off when you're young or you can be financially comfortable when you're a little bit older.

I always took the road of not showing off and never living beyond my means. I wouldn't get credit unless I knew that I could absolutely pay it off within a month—unless, of course, I was buying something I considered an appreciating asset. I have never believed in any type of financing—unless it was real estate or business equipment on which I would get a return. Repeat: Live beneath your means!

Dangers of Debt

The day you turn 18, the credit card companies bombard you with special offers. It's tempting for a young person to go on a spending spree with all of that money that's suddenly available by flashing a piece of plastic. You could have dinner at the best place in town. Buy some stylish clothes. Get the best seats at the next ball game. But this is one of the biggest mistakes you can make.

When you're starting a business you have to be particularly cautious. Debt can be an anchor around your neck. In the long run it does nothing but hold you down. And it can cause undue stress that impacts your health and relationships.

Do I use credit cards? Of course, I do. They're convenient to pay for items I buy online, filling the car up with gas, taking care of the restaurant bill, and so on. But I pay them off at the end of every month. That's positive debt.

Negative debt is when you don't or can't pay them off— because you're probably over-spending on a lifestyle you can't really afford. That's when you are on the road to financial ruin. Headache and heartache await. You won't be able to get out from behind the eight ball. Debt is only to be used in dire circumstances.

So, let's discuss positive debt. What is it? It's a situation where you're borrowing money and you're 99 percent sure that you will be able to make more on the money you borrow than what it's costing you.

Number one on my list of good things to do? As mentioned earlier: buying a house. I certainly don't believe in buying beyond your means, but quite often these days buying a house may well be cheaper than renting. I believe in long-term, fixed-rate mortgages with low interest rates. And be sure to shop around. Check out 30 homes in the same neighborhood and you'll get a pretty good feel for what's a good deal.

If you have an opportunity to buy a commercial property that you're renting it certainly makes more sense to get a mortgage rather than pay the rent. You could find yourself in a situation where your monthly payment on the loan would not be any more (or not much more) than the rent. Why wouldn't you want to take the mortgage? You're building equity. Do that 20 times and you can become rich. (More on this in the chapter on real estate investing).

What about getting a loan to finance the growth of a business venture? Well, if I have signed contacts with people I know and trust, people with whom I've been doing business for a while, I would go to a bank and get debt to finance the growth. That is positive debt or calculated risk debt. Nothing is ever perfect, but if you've educated yourself and know the risks it's worth considering. On the other hand, if someone comes to you with what is obviously a hare-brained, crazy business idea and they want you to loan them money or co-sign, you've got to take a pass.

Repeat: there is negative debt and positive debt. Do not do the negative debt. Do not get into debt to buy yourself a pair of high-end, designer shoes. If you do you're destined to be part of the rat race.

I have a good life now because I was frugal when I was young. I was happy wearing a pair of Levis and a decent shirt and buying my shoes at Costco. I always looked good because I believed looking good was more about taking care of your body, eating well and getting a work-out, rather than buying fancy stuff to show off. I decided when I was in my early twenties that I was going to keep my overhead low so that later in life I would be able to do anything I wanted.

Today, I live like a king. I travel the world. I fly in private jets or first class. I stay in 5-star hotels. I can afford the best cars. That's because I built the foundation of wealth in my younger years. And that is what I am trying to teach in this book.

You might not agree with everything I've written. But realize that I've lived life. I've made mistakes and learned from them. I've had great mentors and learned from them. And it's this accumulated wisdom that I have distilled into these pages. Luckily, I never had to go into great debt to learn these lessons. But I have many friends who did and, believe me, it's better not to embark on that route.

I say again: It's OK to be frugal. Frugal is good. Greed is not good. Do you have the guts to be frugal? Do you have the discipline to be frugal? If you do, it almost certainly means that you're putting money in the bank. You're putting yourself in a position so that when opportunity does knock at your door you will have the financial resources to be able to take advantage of it.

Frugal means taking my own lunch to school or work. Frugal means making my own coffee and not going to a coffee shop. You don't need to keep up with the Joneses. Most millionaires live below their means and that's how they became millionaires.

True success is being strong in mind and body and financially, too.

Don't Gamble

Don't buy lottery tickets. The lottery is run to make a profit, which means that the vast majority of people who play, play to make a loss. On top of that even if you do win, it's probably not going to make you happy. And there are studies to prove that! If you go to Las Vegas to gamble decide your entertainment budget for the trip—and stick to it like glue. Allocate whatever reasonable amount you can afford and when you lose it know for sure that's when you have to be able to walk away. You've had your fun. Don't go and get a cash advance to keep playing the games.

Now a word about education!

Learn a Trade

This might strike you as odd. But I truly believe everyone should learn a trade of some kind. Tradesmen can actually earn a better income than professionals. And you never know when those skills are going to come in useful. The fact that I took auto shop at high school certainly helped me when I opened my smog shop and put my first $50,000 in the bank at the age of 19.

If you're a good tradesman, you can always get a job. It's amazing how many guys I know who started out as a tradesman, whether as a plumber, electrician, auto mechanic, or whatever, then went on to build a good business and ended up buying their location. They then progressed, like me, to make a lot more money buying more real estate. Apart from that, learning a trade is always something to fall back on if times get tough.

I feel so strongly about the issue that I wrote an Op-Ed piece which the Wall Street Journal carried. In it I recalled my time in Auto Shop and made the argument:

I believe that we have the American educational system half wrong. Yes, half of our children need and want the type of education that leads them to higher education. Yet the other half are crammed into a career-learning path that just doesn't work for them or society. Even if they don't drop out, they muddle through without gaining the life skills that will eventually lead them to be productive citizens.

The solution is simple.

In other parts of the World—such as Germany, parts of Scandinavia and regions of Southeast Asia —children are given the choice as early as the sixth grade to follow an academic path or a technical path, thus making sure they are challenged in the appropriate ways and motivated to learn subjects that interest them and prepare them for a career. By ninth grade, students are given a choice whether to get an academic high-school diploma or a technical/vocational high-school diploma.

Imagine what would happen in the U.S. if young men and women were offered interesting, real-life curricula that appealed to them, such as auto shop, computer repair and fashion design. Not only would they learn real-life skills, but along the way they would be taught real-life math. I'm talking about merchant math and accounting, balancing a check book and insurance practices. Classes that would help them achieve their goals of becoming journeymen and skilled labor—which, in many cases and trades—such as computer repair, plumbing and clothing design—might lead them to make a better living than most college graduates.

Now, I am not just calling for the return of shop classes in our schools. Nor am I suggesting that students should stop reading "The Adventures of Huckleberry Finn" and the like. I am calling for complete schools—ones that offer different technical curricula in addition to traditional academic classes. Because when it comes to our education system one size does not fit all. How fair is it that a large portion of children who drop out of high school end up having to go to some vocational school they saw advertised on "Judge Judy" and are thus saddled with large debt?

We can and must do better. I believe that using a school voucher system allowing children to attend this type of school could facilitate the founding of more of them across the country. But however mixed-curricula education is developed—this is how to cut down on the high-school dropout rate. This is how to get more skilled labor. This is how to keep more jobs in America. This is how to build self-esteem and educate children who go on to create businesses that employ America.

Do's and Don'ts

Here's a handy checklist of some financial things you should do and some you definitely shouldn't do.

Do - Pay off credit cards at the end of the month.

Don't - buy or rent furniture, electronics, etc. on credit

Do - Get credit cards with the lowest rates. (If you are going to carry debt – shop the rate).

Do - Get credit cards and ATM cards with no foreign exchange rate fee if you're going to travel internationally.

Don't - Buy a fancy car on credit.

Do - Try to pay cash for a 1-2 year old car and keep the car for five years (or longer).

Don't - Spend beyond your means and if you can't control yourself, cut up your credit card.

Do - Shop at discount warehouse stores.

Don't - Shop at fancy mall stores (unless there's a big sale).

Do - Know where the cheapest gas is sold and fill up when it's on your way.

Do - Consider gas mileage when buying a vehicle.

Do - Consider a smaller motor (four cylinder or hybrid).

Don't - Buy the extended warranty.

Do - Self-insure when feasible.

Do - Only buy TERM life insurance.

Do - Have the guts to shop at good thrift stores.

Do - Have the guts to make and bring your own lunch.

Do - Have the discipline to make water your drink of choice.

Don't - Eat out.

Don't - Waste your money in bars or coffee shops.

Don't - Waste water, gas, and electricity.

Do - Turn your water heater down.

Don't - Valet park.

Do - Comparison shop before you buy (especially for cars and appliances).

Don't - Smoke (it's not only expensive but will also killing you).

Don't - Gamble (or if you're going to, have a budget and stick to it).

Don't - Use cash advance machines that charge exorbitant fees.

Don't - Use the check cashing pay day loan services.

Do - Have your coffee at home or the office.

Do - Buy things on sale.

Do - Always ask at the box office, are there any specials I should know about?

Do - Bring water and peanuts to the game.

Chapter 11. Make It Happen Bigger

How big to you want to be? I find it hard to believe that anyone would start a business with the attitude 'I want to be a little guy. I just want a really small business.' It's in the nature of hard-charging entrepreneurs to keep building and growing. The more successful you become, the more you can help other people become successful. In this chapter I want to share some advice for building a bigger business.

Find People You Can Trust

You can't build a large company all by yourself. You need a team. You can't scale without people you can completely trust. It's like trying to build a house on a lousy foundation. If the foundation is not solid the house will crumble.

You need relationships with people of integrity inside and outside the company, whether people on your staff or suppliers. These relationships don't come fast. They just come with experience, knowledge, and time.

There are some guys with whom I've done business and I know I could trust them with my entire estate. There are others—well, enough said. You deal with the good guys for long-term success. Even if you have to pay more—it's worth it.

It's vital to work with like-minded people; kindred souls. Let me give you an example. About 15 years ago I met some young guys at the gym and we became great friends. They ended up founding a multi-billion dollar company. They are still my dear friends and they have introduced me to other people who have become business associates and others who have become sensational employees.

Their success has become my success and my success has become their success. When you have friends such as this who are on the same path in life and are achievers it makes it easier to create your own luck. When you mix with people who have the same mindset—especially if they are at the gym, playing golf or tennis rather than at the bar drinking—you can do wonderful things together.

I have a history of being at the right place at the right time because of living the type of lifestyle that I live. It's not difficult, but it does take commitment.

Work With Winners

Perhaps this is a statement of the obvious! And I touched on this point earlier. But why would you want to work with losers? Surround yourself with people who have the same winning attitude that you have, and you can't go far wrong. That goes for investing as well. Don't give your hard-earned money to someone who doesn't have a solid track record of getting good returns.

How To Hire

You have to have a secure ego that enables you to hire the best talent. It's one of the most important things you can do. You hire great people and let them do their job.

How do you find them from the hundreds of seemingly well-qualified candidates?

First of all don't underestimate the importance of scrutinizing resumes and checking references.

Resumes: It's a real turn-off for me when I see that someone has had multiple jobs lasting less than 18 months.

That's a red flag. I can't build a business relying on people who jump around like that. I want people who recognize that I'm giving them a great opportunity and a great financial package and will want to be part of my team long-term. I want people who share my vision and my passion and have the same work ethic. I value loyalty.

References: Don't take them at face value. You can't shortcut this. You need to check out the references and talk with them. Especially when you're considering someone for a senior position. Have a detailed conversation. If references don't return your phone call it's not a good sign. They're avoiding you for a reason. Make sure that you check with the candidate's most recent employer. If someone did a good job for me I like to be a good reference. And it's dumb anyway to give someone as a reference if you're not sure they will give you a rousing endorsement!

Test: Yes, you can test the skills of someone who wants a job. Make sure that, for instance, they are truly proficient in any computer skills that they may claim to have mastered. Make it clear upfront that someone will begin work on a trial basis. If they do a good job—they will keep it. If not—you will have to let them go. I usually make sure that newcomers are aware that I have a 90-day evaluation period.

How To Fire

Knowing when to hire is one thing; knowing when to fire is something else. And a whole lot harder. One smart high-tech business leader said that if he couldn't look at someone after 90 days (or less) and say that he would rehire him (or her) then he lets them go. I agree. You have to have the guts to do this. You can't afford to be complacent and let the wrong people languish in their jobs, especially if they are holding pivotal positions. Often letting someone go is right for them, too. So for the welfare of your business, you sometimes have to bite the bullet and do the tough thing.

I like to give people one or two chances. But if you see them making bad decisions or they're chronically late to work, don't waste your time. Cut the cord and find someone who values working for you.

And when you have to fire someone—keep it short and sweet. Don't go into all of the reasons. Unfortunately, because of the potential legal ramifications I don't normally give counseling on why someone is not performing. Even if they have behaved abysmally I don't want to create animosity because you never know when it's going to come back to haunt you. I do, however, like to be very fair with severance even if I really think an individual doesn't deserve anything. Personally, I don't want the hassle. That's just the way it is.

Sometimes it's not so difficult to let someone go. Let me give you an example. We decided at Auction.com that we wanted to supply fresh fruit for our employees. One of the employees who handled facilities was tasked with getting us a great deal. He presented what he thought was a great deal. It was a source that was certainly 30 percent cheaper than Harry and David which is a delicious first class brand. But it was still going to cost us about $160,000 a year, which seemed ridiculously high to me. This guy didn't know me too well because I simply picked up the phone, called a fruit wholesaler that supplies restaurants, and got the same kind of fruit (albeit in smaller sizes) for about $15,000 a year. This guy was going to spend 10 times as

much. Needless to say he doesn't work for me any more.
But the point here is that to be a good executive you should
spend your company's money as if it were your own
money.

Let me give you another example—this time a positive
one. About 20 years ago the husband of one of our
employees came to one of our land auctions. He was a
young Marine named Walter Skrzynski. And instead of just
hanging around watching what was going on, as a typical
gung-ho Marine he jumped in to help. Whenever he saw
something that needed doing, he did it. He wasn't even on
the payroll. Pretty soon we gave him a part-time job. We
grabbed his services whenever we could because there's
always a place for hard-workers who take the initiative. We
knew he was going to put in all of his 20 years with the
Marines—he had about 10 left to go—but we made it clear
there was always a position waiting for him. It actually
became a running joke with us: How many years do you
have left?

Walter had enlisted with the Marine Corps at the age of 17
and when he retired with the rank of Major we gave him
that full-time position and he basically started the next day!
He went on to recruit many other retired Marines,
particularly officers, into the company. A great bunch of
guys with a wonderful work ethic who know how to lead a
team. Funnily enough, although we hired a lot of superb
officers our former president Jim Corum, for whom I have
a lot of respect and who helped build the business, was
actually a retired Master Sergeant! Walter, however, is
another great leader who is still with us today as our
Executive Vice President and still a hard-worker who takes
the initiative just like that young Marine I first met.

Why Some Businesses Fail, Why Some Businesses Succeed

What makes the difference between success and failure? Over the years I've come to recognize some common factors.

One of the key reasons a business fails is because it doesn't deliver good old-fashioned customer service. This boils down to some very basic elements. Do you return calls promptly? Do you show up for appointments on time? Do you get the work done as scheduled? Do you deliver more than what was agreed upon? Is the quality of your work top-notch the first time around?

When people take shortcuts in business they think they are getting away with something, but in the long run it's the road to ruin. You'll get bad word-of-mouth and you won't get repeat business and personal referrals, the two most inexpensive forms of business generation.

Businesses today are exposed like never before because customers can publicly rate you on the Internet for all the world to see. Lousy service will get you embarrassingly bad and business-destroying reviews.

Treat people like you'd treat your mother. Greet people like you'd greet a friend. Charge a fair price for an honest day's work or a fair price for an honest product and people will give you business again and again.

As your business grows constantly monitor that all of your employees share your philosophy. Email surveys to your customers asking, "How did we do?" If your survey flushes out a bad apple employee, don't hesitate to let them go. Don't let one person ruin your reputation. Shop your own business. By that I mean you should call your company as if you were a client and see what kind of response you get—or send in a professional shopper to investigate for you. Have your customer service calls recorded and listen to them. You need the inside track on how your company looks to the outside. Also check sites like Yelp and Glassdoor to see what people are saying about you.

Once you build the foundation of delivering quality work at a fair price and treating people well you have to advertise. As I've mentioned elsewhere you can construct a professional website quite inexpensively. You can advertise using Craigslist and other online sources for free. Let me reiterate: You have to advertise and you have to track. You have to know what's working and what's not working.

I've had a lot of businesses that have failed. It was probably my fault or maybe it was just not the right time or right place. If I feel a business is not getting traction in three to six months I'm ready to shut it down. I know that sounds really fast, but if business is bad and there's no foot traffic I move on.

Here's an example. We shot a TV infomercial for a product that I thought had a lot of potential. It was a mineral in a packet that you put in the refrigerator to keep your food fresher. When we aired it, we only got one or two phone calls whereas we needed more like 100 calls for it to have been deemed a success. We tested it several times but the results were just as abysmal. Evidently the market didn't want this wonderful product so we just accepted that it was a failure and called it a day. We didn't beat ourselves up. It was a test. It didn't work. Next!

What disappoints me is when people do stupid things. They don't open their store on time or they don't return phone calls promptly. If it's a restaurant and they don't clear dirty dishes from the table or the bathroom is filthy what kind of signal does that send? It upsets me when people dress slovenly or have alcohol on their breath. Not good messages. You really have to put your best foot forward at all times. Not just now and then, but every day. If it's your business make sure it doesn't fail because you do something stupid. If you don't care why should anyone else care?

Leadership Traits

So what does it take to be a business leader? There are some common attributes that you can find in anyone who successfully spearheads any kind of large organization.

A leader is someone willing to make decisions.

A leader is the first in and the last to leave until he can pass the mantle to another strong leader willing to take over and do exactly same thing.

A leader praises in public and chastises in private.

A leader leads by acting the way he wants his employees to act.

A leader doesn't allow harassment or discrimination. It's something we don't tolerate in our businesses from the highest levels.

A leader sets good lifestyle examples. One of the reasons I talk so much about health in this book is because we have been given this great gift of life and I hate to see someone abuse it and self-inflict damage to the bodies God gave us. So I lead by example by not smoking and by exercising to keeping myself in good shape and having good personal hygiene.

A leader keeps an open mind and doesn't have to be right all the time. He asks for opinions and debates everything and then decides the right course of action.

A leader is willing to change his mind if someone has a better idea.

A leader doesn't need to be the one with the great idea. He is not a glory hog. He will give most of the credit to those who work for him. He will let the team be the winner. He is humble and gets the job done.

If you want to build a world-class business these are among the leadership traits you need to foster.

Keep Up With Tech

In today's fast-paced, high-tech world the only constant is change. One of the most powerful tools at our disposal is the computer. So, this piece of advice might sound like basic common sense. But that doesn't make it any less important for me to emphasize the need not only to acquire computer skills, but also to continue to master new computer skills.

You have to keep up to date with technology.

I was blessed to learn at an early age the value of computer skills. I had friends who taught me, for instance, how to do mail merges so I could efficiently send the same letter to masses of people.

Even if you're not expert you need to know enough about what computers can do so that you can talk intelligently to the experts and get maximum performance out of them. You have to know enough so that no-one can bullshit you.

I always like to hire people that have comprehensive computer skills because they can always accomplish more in a shorter period of time. If you realize that you aren't as computer-savvy as you'd like to be you can easily become much more proficient by taking just 10 to 20 hours of computer classes. It's a valuable investment of your time.

As an entrepreneur it's important that you make the effort to learn about databases; how Microsoft Office works; Google searches; etc. Learn what a computer can do. You can't always expect your employees to do it for you.

Negotiating 101

There are a lot of great books about the art of negotiating, so I will keep this section short and highlight just a few key points.

Point number one is that you always want the opposing negotiator to make the first offer whether you're buying or selling. Their first number might be better than what you'd anticipated. So, make them go first. And, regardless of the number, you always have to hem and haw and counter offer, even if your counter is just a fraction less. If you immediately jump on their offer they may well quickly conclude that they got the number wrong and promptly back out of the deal. So, even if you loved the number don't show it. Make the other person feel good about the deal.

One of the reasons why many kids from overseas are better entrepreneurs than those born and raised in the states is because they come from a country and a culture where everything is a negotiation. It's second nature to them. It's normal every day behavior. "Haggling" is normal. In the states you can easily practice your negotiating skills by going to a swap meet and haggling there. Just like I did when I was a kid.

And there's much more to good financial health—as we'll see in the next chapter.

Chapter 12. Personal Finances

Manage your money wisely. Be prudent. Look to the future. Think about your retirement from an early age. If this sounds like good commonsense advice (like most of the advice in this book) that's because it is. But it's amazing how many people stray from a sensible financial course. So here are some tips on handling your personal finances.

Know What You Make

Do you really know how much you earn? How much actually goes into your pocket—after all of the taxes? In other words what cash is available for you to invest and support your lifestyle? What's that number on an hourly basis? Think about that amount whenever you're about to make a purchase. Is that dinner at a great restaurant or yet another pair of black shoes really worth one day's pay?

Know What Works For You

Always develop a financial strategy that matches your personality and temperament and/or find an expert you can really trust. The bottom line: if you're not a details person it doesn't make sense for you to undertake complicated financial or tax strategies. If you're an unashamed shopaholic and can't resist something on sale, shred those plastic cards that make impulse purchases all too easy.

Simply The Best

The most effective strategy of all: put together a simple, diversified portfolio of low-cost index funds. Rebalance them on an annual basis. Avoid complex investment strategies that, to be honest, are mostly designed to generate commissions for brokers.

Buy Equities

The best long-term returns come from equities, typically 4 percent to 5 percent a year above inflation. So most of your long-term portfolio should be invested in low-cost ETFs.

Picking Stocks

Be wary of buying individual stocks unless you view it as an out-and-out gamble. Don't pick a stock just because it's the hottest word-of-mouth thing around and the buzz is that it's guaranteed to skyrocket. Don't pay attention to the so-called Wall Street experts. Their hot picks, on average, rarely perform any better than random picks. And be careful of putting money into your employer's stock. Your job is probably enough financial exposure riding on one horse.
Treasuries Ring True
Balance your portfolio with some long-term Treasury bonds and Treasury inflation-protected securities. Chances are their values will hold true, and possibly increase, when stocks crash.

Inside Insurance

Insurance is a necessary evil. But it's usually costly. Regardless of whether you're taking out coverage for your home or your car getting a high-deductible is usually the safer bet. One good purchase: disability coverage—just in case disaster hits. And, similarly, get term life insurance, so your dependents are helped in the event of your untimely demise. You can shop online and buy wholesale.

Plan For The Future

As I've said before you're never too young to start saving for the future—stashing away as much as you can. Look at it this way. If you invest a dollar for four years at an interest rate of 4 percent you'll accumulate $1.50. On the other hand, if you leave it there for 40 years, you'll have nearly $5.00. Which amount would you rather have going into your retirement?

In fact, a third of your entire life could come after the age of 65. So you should definitely try to pay off your mortgage and save a minimum of 10 times your annual salary so you can enjoy a comfortable retirement. And when it comes to Social Security: delay taking it for as long as you can up to the age of 70 so you can get a bigger monthly check.

Living The Lottery

What do I mean by "living the lottery?" It's living your life in the hope that you're going to get some kind of windfall that will solve all of your financial problems. I don't literally mean the lottery. I'm thinking of the expectation of something like a pay raise, stock windfall or inheritance. An influx of cash of that kind. Learn to live with what you have. There's an old saying worth repeating: A rich man is the one who's satisfied with what he has.

And while on the subject of living with what you have… you can always live without some things. Take a look at your monthly budget and see what indulgences or extravagances can be trimmed. Most smartphone bills are too high. Most cable bills are too high (do you really need all of those channels?). Most folks spend too much on their cars. Where can you cut?

Conserve and Protect

Hopefully, you will build a nest egg. It's there for your golden years, once you've retired. It's not there to pay for your children's college education. Your 401(k) or IRAs are not there to cash in (and incur taxes and penalties) so you can launch a new business venture. Also bear in mind that if they're in shelters, your nest egg is protected from creditors. You should have contributed as much as possible to your company's 401(k) plan—at least enough to get the company matching amount.

Teach Your Children Well

One of the greatest gifts you can give your offspring is how to handle money responsibly. It's your responsibility— no-one else's. It's one of the best lessons in life that they will need every day of their life. Please tell them when they're young about the value of owning real estate.

Chapter 13. Real Estate Riches

Investing in real estate is one of the surest and easiest ways to make your fortune. Just look at history. In general, since the 1800s real estate prices have increased steadily. Yes, there have been periods of increases and decreases, and periods of more or less demand for housing, but the overall trend has been dynamically upwards.

Even after the housing market collapse of 2008, real estate prices have bounced back in almost every part of the country. Combined with the fact that you can purchase property with little money down, the average annual rate increase alone—about 5 percent per year over the past 20 years—makes real property my favorite investment.

So much so that in addition to the success of Auction.com, which has sold over $37 billion worth of real estate, I personally own properties including homes, apartment buildings, office buildings, retail centers and more.

But real estate investing is not a get-rich-quick deal; typically, it's a get-rich-slow deal. It is a matter of planting seeds that you harvest many years later. Plant enough seeds and you'll harvest a lot of profit—in the long term. It's also a matter of taking the time to thoroughly educate yourself and research the real estate market before investing a penny. Knowledge is power.

I've principally made money in real estate by buying and holding property. Some I've never sold; others I've adopted a "buy-fix-and-hold strategy." In this approach an investor purchases an existing home at a good price and then fixes it up and rents it out. Over time, the appreciation (and other financial benefits) allows you to build wealth. You still need money to purchase the property, renovate it, and endure any expenses associated with rental property. But this is a proven, tried and true method of building one's financial nest egg over time using someone else's rent money to pay for your mortgage. You can probably refinance, too, and further improve your bottom line.

The other approach is the "buy-and-flip strategy." Here, the investor purchases an existing home, improves it, and then sells it or "flips" it to a buyer at full market value (retail) price. You need money to purchase the property, renovate it, pay the bills for the duration of the project, and sell it. Some people do that all the time, and do very nicely.

Own Your Commercial Building

Most businesses need real estate. It makes sense, therefore, to try and own the building that houses your business. That's what I've done and, in many instances, I've made more money from owning the property than I did from running the business.

I discussed earlier how in my younger years I opened the small chain of consumer electronics stores. It was an interesting experience (and gave me an aversion to retail). But the smartest thing I did was find a great location. The property, however, was closed down and there was no 'for sale' sign anywhere to be seen. I tracked down the owner from the tax records and I kept bugging him until he finally sold the property to me.

I paid about $375,000. I had the retail business there for two or three years. But, as I mentioned earlier, I own the real estate to this day. The rent has probably paid for the building five times over. If you have a solid business, then buying the real estate and being your own landlord is a sensational way to make money.

I highly recommend that, if you can, always get an option to buy when you lease property so that you can acquire it when your business becomes successful. You can wake up 10 to 15 years later and you own the property. You will have made the profit rather than the landlord. This is something you should do if you have a business that needs commercial space. It's a no-brainer.

Check out the U.S. Small Business Administration. The SBA participates in a number of loan programs designed for business owners who may have difficulty getting a traditional bank loan—and you may well qualify.

Bigger Is Better

You should also consider purchasing a commercial property that's bigger than the needs of your business. Rent out the extra space and it will help pay your mortgage. This has been a model that's worked very well for me. It may sound a little daunting, but it's not. Just take one step at a time and you'll succeed. But you have to educate yourself along the way. Do your homework. Investigate many properties. Get on the email lists of local real estate agents. Get an idea of the true value of the properties so that you'll recognize a good deal when it comes along and you'll be able to hop right on it. Read books. Read online articles. Take a night course. Buy DVDs (Look on eBay. You can find courses that sold through TV infomercials for $200.00 for just $20.00 to $30.00!). Do whatever it takes.

Rental Income

Timing is everything. Play your cards right and invest at the right time. Let's say there's a growing market for

houses. Population is expanding. You know an area that's
hot for commuters and maybe you can buy homes for as
little as $100,000. Rent them out and there's a good chance
the rental income will cover your mortgage. Meanwhile
you have an asset that over the years—and especially in the
long haul—is going to increase in value. It's still a risk.
Any debt is risk. But it's a calculated risk. And that's how
hundreds of thousands of people around the planet have
become rich.

Location. Location. Location.

We've talked about "location, location, location." It's a
given in the real estate world. But there's more to it than
that. When I buy a piece of real estate I want to know a) Is
it a good location? and b) If the right business goes in that
location will it stay rented? That's why, even as a landlord
I'm reluctant to rent to a business owner if I don't feel the
property is suitable for their business. I want them to
succeed. (And I want them to be a long-term tenant).
  Let me give you an example of a good location: the
location for our first stereo store was perfect. It was
situated right on a signalized corner. It had high visibility. A
corner location is a prime location.
  And an example of a bad location: I live in a little town
on the beach and someone opened up a shop that sold these
really delicious cupcakes. It was located in the downtown
area but you had to go out of your way to find it. My first
thought: Fabulous product. Lousy location. When it comes
to consumables like cupcakes or cookies or ice cream or
yogurt you need a lot of walk-by traffic. You want people
to see and smell what you have on offer so they are likely
to make an instant decision to buy. Ultimately, that business

had to be moved. I'm sure it must have cost them $100,000. I have no doubt that if the store had been on the main drag it would have done fabulously well.

Making the right decisions can build foundational wealth. You've just go to have the determination to do it. Let me reiterate: First you look for the right kind of real estate. Second, make sure it's a good location. Third, be ready to identify and grab the right deal. When you've looked at enough properties and talked to enough people you'll know good value when you see it. Don't count on others to do it for you. Educate yourself. It's not that hard.

Think hard about location. If you have a foot massage business wouldn't it make sense to situate it in an area where a large number of people are walking by? If you have an auto-repair shop wouldn't you want to have it located where a lot of people are driving their cars? You have to be seen in a location that's most appropriate for the kind of business you are running.

Mastering Auctions

I'm obviously one of the world's biggest supporters of selling real estate by way of auctions! There are several key benefits whether the auctions are online or held live, in person.

First, you are in control. You can always walk away from the deal during the bidding process if you don't think you'll obtain your required profit margin on the property.

Second, it's transparent. There are no "inside deals" or monkey business—there is a level playing field for all investors.

Third, it's efficient; there are no time-consuming "back and forth" negotiations between the buyer, seller and realtor. You won't have to wait days or even weeks for the buyer to present a counter offer. With an auction, you'll know the final selling price of a property right away, usually within a few minutes.

The number of real estate auctions has grown in recent years because investors are beginning to realize that auctions have revolutionized the real estate business. An auction provides both buyers and sellers with timely, successful results. Sellers get an offer under a competitive bidding scenario. Buyers arrive both informed and motivated. Therefore, they save on the carrying costs normally associated with selling property—interest, real estate taxes, and maintenance.

If you are used to buying and selling property in negotiated, fixed transactions, the atmosphere of an auction may be a jolt. The value consensus, normally haggled over during a series of time-consuming exchanges, becomes based only on one thing: what someone is willing to pay at that very moment. In this way, at an auction, value is determined by price.

Keep To Your Goal

An ideal investor has a laser focus on their goal. You have done your research and you know exactly what the property is worth. You work out the return you want on every investment. Keep that goal in the front of your mind and refuse to settle for less. If the price doesn't match your valuation and profit goals, let it go and wait for the next one…it's out there.

This gives you an edge over your competitors because you will know exactly what the property is truly worth— and you'll know when you've bid far enough. For example,

let's say that a piece of land is zoned agricultural, and all
the other potential buyers are bidding as if it's intended for
agricultural use. But you have done your research and you
know that it's perfect for a shopping center. Knowing the
potential return on this investment, you know that it's okay
to bid up to a higher price.

Be Creative

Try to think outside the box in a very creative way every
time you look at a piece of property.

Creativity means more than just trying to come up with an
idea that's different from the norm. Creativity means
solving a problem in a new and unique way—departing
from the "normal" solution.

Most of us have had our creative side stifled in one way
or another. Typical parenting and educational systems
program us to act in a conventional way—the same as
everybody else. But if you're going to make money at real
estate, you must step beyond the "everybody else"
mentality. Instead, be fearless in your willingness to depart
from the typical, conventional way of purchasing,
financing, and selling. In order to do this you will have to
let go of the past, and possibly other people's opinions
about you. You will have to silence that "little voice" in
your head that says you can't do it—because you can.

Once you have re-trained yourself to think differently
about the various financial solutions and the many possible
uses for property, it will become easy and fun. You will be
unconventional—but you'll have more money in your
pocket than people who only seek conventional financing
and who are not risk-takers. If you ultimately are making
more money than people who choose to only look for

normal solutions to problems, who want to "play it safe" — then you won't be considered eccentric — you will be seen as exceptional.

By the way, it is important to keep in mind that there is no such thing as a perfect marketplace. If you are waiting for "everything" to fall into place, you will never purchase anything at all. No two properties are alike, and the only question is: how is this property going to make money for me?

What will you do when you've acquired wealth through real estate? In my case I love to travel and I love to be able to support worthy causes. I tackle both of these subjects in the following two chapters.

Chapter 14. The Joy of Travel

Traveling is really important. It can open your mind to new experiences. You can see how other people around the world do different things and do things differently. And, yes, sometimes they even do them better than we do in America.

If you're going to start any business I would always recommend that you go look at that business not only in other parts of the country, but also in other parts of the world, and learn from what they're doing. I wrote earlier in the book about the visit Jeff and I made to Australia and New Zealand when we were researching the auction business and the wealth of knowledge we acquired.

Based on my visits to many countries I'd like to share with you some useful tips for being a smart traveler whether you're on a business trip or vacationing with your family and friends. Here are some rules—in no particular order of significance.

Rule Number 1. Don't take expensive jewelry. The only items of value you really need are your computer and your phone. I don't wear fancy watches. In fact, I don't wear any jewelry when I travel overseas. I dress down as much as possible. I just don't want to stand out and make myself a target in any way.

Rule Number 2. Learn a few words in the language of the country you're visiting. A few words of greeting and expressions of appreciation make a big difference. Typically, when people see that you've made an effort to pick up their language you will get an even warmer welcome. And always greet people with a smile.

Rule Number 3. When you get into a taxi, always make the driver switch on the meter. If they don't have a meter, ask them the price up-front. If they don't want to use the meter or don't want to give you a guaranteed price, give them a wide berth and find another car. Otherwise, you are 100 percent guaranteed of a hassle later.

Rule Number 4. Make several copies of your passport and keep them in separate bags. You never know when you might need to prove your identity and, in the worst case scenario, replace a lost or stolen passport.

Rule Number 5. When you leave your hotel room leave most of your money and credit cards in the safe (assuming you're in a decent enough hotel that has one in the room). The last thing you want to have happen is get robbed and lose everything!

Rule Number 6. Get the best exchange rate for your money—whether getting cash or using your credit card. The bank ATM is almost certainly better than those currency exchange bureaus you see at major tourist spots. Before you travel, check to see the different percentages that might be charged as a service fee for using any particular card. Some banks charge 2-3 percent; others zero or 1 percent. It's better than taking cash in hard dollars and trying to exchange that. I have a Fidelity ATM card and it's no-cost. They don't charge any fee to do the exchange, so I'm getting the absolute best rate. You can save a lot of money by using the right card.

Many credit cards charge as much as a 3 percent exchange rate fee. So, in other words, if you go to obtain

$100.00 worth of foreign currency at the ATM, they actually only give you $97.00 of that currency.

Beware of super high fees at airport exchange bureaus. You pay for the convenience. It might look like you're getting a fantastic exchange rate until you read the small print. Perhaps you've heard the expression: What the big font giveth, the small font taketh away. In this case the small print reveals the fee that they charge above the exchange rate.

Rule Number 7. If you're hiring a guide get the price up-front and, if possible, use people who are licensed. In many countries that I've visited there are licensed guides who literally went to college to become accredited as a guide. Not only are they more professional but also are often no more expensive than non-licensed, potentially unscrupulous individuals.

Rule Number 8. Drink bottled water—especially if you're in a third world country. Alternatively, boil the water. Hotel rooms often come with a tea kettle so just boil all your water and use it for brushing your teeth and rinsing your mouth, as well as for drinking.

Rule Number 9. Hide your money. Always carry your cash in your front pocket. I've experienced an attempted pick-pocketing and once suffered a mugging, but the criminals didn't get anything because all of my valuables were in my front pocket.

Let me share with you a couple of interesting situations from my travels. On one occasion I was walking down the famous Ipanema beach in Rio de Janeiro when I noticed something that looked very much like dog poop on my shoe. Immediately, a young man came up to me and said, "Oh sir, a dog has pooped on your shoe. Would you like me to clean it?"

He held up his shoe shine box and I thought, Oh sure. Why not? It took him all of 45 seconds to "clean" my shoes whereupon he turned his box around to reveal the sign declaring, "Shoe Shine $20." As soon as I told him he was crazy, I was surrounded by seven or eight 18- to 20-year-old thugs. The funny thing is that for some reason I really wasn't carrying any money that day. I only had a few dollars in my pockets, which I was happy to show them and walk away. But it was another form of mugging. Obviously this was a little con that these guys used. They spray something on your shoe and then they play this intimidation game.

The second time something like this happened to me I was in Budapest, Hungary with my former wife. We went into the subway and got on a car which was almost empty. But then, all of a sudden, a whole group of people got onto the same car, surrounding and crowding us. I quickly covered my money and my bag and it felt like we were getting a quick frisking but they figured just as quickly that they couldn't pickpocket us and were off the train before it even left the station.

Rule Number 10. Be careful when paying a restaurant bill. The menu will be in the local currency. But when they're about to bring you the bill they might ask if you'd like it in American dollars. Assuming you say yes, the chances are that you won't get the proper exchange rate. So let's say, for example, the Thai baht is at 33, but when they exchange it they're only going to give you 30. Forget it. Just tell them to keep the bill in their currency and use your credit card. Then you know you will get the proper wholesale exchange rate, and they can't take advantage of you.

I've been in restaurants in Mexico where they were helping themselves to a 15 percent exchange rate fee, so if I was supposed to be getting 15 pesos to the dollar when they brought me the bill I was actually only getting 12.75 pesos to the dollar. Most people are not astute enough to do that math that fast on the fly. So, it's better to leave the bill in the currency of the country you're visiting.

Rule Number 11. Now let's talk about airlines. I'm blessed to say that these days I get to travel business class or first class, but there are so many different airlines and the prices vary so much that you really have to shop around. Whether you're flying first, business or economy check all of your options, otherwise you could pay twice as much as necessary.

The quality of an airline's food on the airplane is not my top priority, but a good, clean plane with a lie-down bed—that's important on long haul flights. When I was on long flights in coach I would always try to secure an emergency exit seat or sometimes a seat in the bulk-head, with extra legroom. Comfort is what matters to me. I always check seatguru.com to see what kind of seat I'm getting.

More than anything else, though, I'm concerned about the length of a flight—especially international—and getting to my destination in the fastest possible time. If you're not careful lay-overs can add hours and hours to your trip.

Rule Number 12. Avoid getting lost! These days you can always get directions on your smartphone or iPad. I still like to use the Garmin because it just seems to be easier and they've got a great little kit to put right into the rental car or carry around with you. I like to pre-program it before I leave the states. I enter the hotels I'm going to be staying at and major points of interest. Of course, there are times when I still get lost but the program always gets me back on course without any stress. And besides "getting lost" is all part of the fun and adventure that is travel.

Rule Number 13. Check out websites like TripAdvisor. You'll read reviews and ratings of all kinds of places to stay that are more interesting than the familiarity of a Hilton or a Marriot. With the big name international chains you know exactly what you're going to get…but sometimes it's more fun to do something a little offbeat. Shop around online.

Rule Number 14. Beat the language barrier. Let's say you arrive at another country—especially one where the language is completely "alien" to the western eye—Russia or China, for example. You'll often find that there are translators at the airport who will write simple messages for you.

When I was in China I had a great tour guide who spoke excellent English, and I would videotape her saying a message that I wanted to communicate later—perhaps directions for a taxi driver. All I had to do was show the driver the tape!

You don't have to be rich to travel. Traveling is good—at every level. If you can't afford first class air fares and five-star hotels you can always take trains, use a backpack and stay at hostels. It's fun and it's educational. At every age. But the sooner you start, the younger you start, the better it is. It's good for young people to go figure it out.

Traveling is a learning experience. It opens your eyes to all aspects of this wonderful world we inhabit. There are so many different cultures, different foods, and different languages. Encountering and embracing them broadens your horizons. Traveling has made me a better business person, and I believe traveling will make you a better business person. Most people on this planet are good people. Be good to them and they will be good to you. Have fun. Happy travels.

Chapter 15. The Joy of Giving

I believe in giving back. I've been extremely fortunate to become successful and more than comfortable financially. And I want to do whatever I can to make a difference in the lives of others. If you have charitable donations as a low priority on your budget I urge you to take another long, hard look at your budget. Think again, and help a worthy cause—or causes. Choose something that has personal meaning to you.

For me my 25 year involvement with Big Brothers Big Sisters of Orange County has brought great joy and immense satisfaction into my life.

I can honestly tell you that when I'm involved in a major business project and things aren't going my way I can switch my thoughts to the 2,500 kids that we serve in Orange County and it immediately brightens my day. It scatters any clouds hanging over me and lets the sunshine in. It makes me happy. I know I'm doing good. And when I'm happy I do better in my personal relationships; I do better in my business deals. You can't beat the gratification of being in service to others.

I've not only given my time mentoring kids and the organization itself but also—thanks to my financial success —have been blessed to be able to make donations so that Big Brothers Big Sisters could expand its mentorship program to help children realize their potential and build their own future. I've also focused on supporting the organization's "Big" recruitment campaign, which aims to find dynamic and committed male volunteers for male "Littles" which is one of the organization's biggest needs.

I don't do it for recognition but I have to say that in 2014 I was so honored when Big Brothers Big Sisters of Orange

County presented me with the Joel K. Rubenstein award. It's an award that's given to those who have demonstrated loyal and profound passion for the nonprofit group and made a lasting and permanent impact.

Why Big Brothers Big Sisters? Why did I choose to become a board member 25 years ago when I could have supported any worthy nonprofit?

Their core mission struck a chord with me. Big Brothers Big Sisters believes that every child has the ability to succeed and thrive in life. Most of the kids the organization mentors come from single-parent and low-income families or households where a parent is in jail. Studies have shown that Big Brothers Big Sisters relationships' with children improves their chances of performing better in school and steering clear of violence and crime as well as developing stronger relationships with their parents. If you tackle problems when they're young these kids have a chance of becoming adults who make a positive contribution.

I have one of my mentors to thank for the introduction to Big Brothers Big Sisters. It came about because someone had donated land to the organization and they brought it to us to put it up for auction. We successfully sold the land but felt we had made too much money on the deal. At that time we owned thee Volkswagen dealership so we decided to make our own contribution by donating a new VW for their next big auction.

It wasn't long before I came to an appreciation of just what a remarkable organization this was. I totally believe in solving issues with kids when they're young so they don't manifest into lifelong problems. So I became actively involved and my passion remains recruiting "Bigs"—other guys to mentor and inspire kids that come from a challenging environment.

Some years ago another friend introduced me to India and I've been infatuated with the country ever since and try to help children there as much as I can. India is probably the most fascinating place on the planet. I have a love hate relationship with the country.

One of the things I love is that most educated people speak English so, although it's obviously a very different culture, you can still walk the streets and talk to people. Of course, what I hate is that it's a country with such abject poverty. There is such a lack of funding for everything, but particularly education.

When I decided that I wanted to help in some small way I hired a guy to tour the country and research schools that were doing a good job but were in desperate need of funding. He came back with five different charities and I decided to help two of them, Romana's Garden in Rishikesh and Him Jyoti in Dehradun.

The lady at Romana's Garden adopted 60 children and runs the place on a shoestring. I felt she was so worthy of a contribution.

The best model of all, though, is Him Jyoti, a free boarding school for underprivileged girls started by Sudarshan Agarwal, former Governor of the state of Uttarakhand. His mission was to find young girls that showed the most promise; that had the greatest hunger for education. He visited village schools, some of them in the mountains where there was no running water and extreme poverty, to find them. Today there are 200 girls getting full board and committed to learning so they can make their way in the world.

I not only financially support them but also visit once or twice a year to give my time and share my experiences and provide input. I've talked to these girls about the fact that it is definitely not acceptable for men to beat women, something which happens all too often in their culture. I've talked with them, too, concerning the awful amount of trash that is just thrown everywhere and what a health hazard it is. I've heard it said in India that it's acceptable to discard trash because it gives a job to someone of a lower caste. I've tried to change that thinking and emphasize that cleanliness is next to Godliness. All of these lessons are so that the girls can go back to their villages, believing in themselves and better equipped to become educated leaders in their communities.

I urge you to find a charitable cause that's close to your heart and make whatever contribution you can, whether time or money. There are deserving people in your neighborhood and neighborhoods across the world who are less fortunate. Make a commitment to make a difference.

Chapter 16. Take-Away Advice

Congratulations. You've made it to the end of my book. And I trust I've achieved my goal of sharing solid, commonsense business strategies and lessons from my personal experiences so that you can learn from them.

I've been an entrepreneur for as long as I can remember. As I said at the beginning: doing deals and real estate seems to be in my DNA. I've had a very eclectic business journey. I've done so many different things and I've had a life that's been rich in so many ways. I've kind of always done what I've wanted to do. And that's one important lesson because you'll never be successful unless you're wildly enthusiastic about your chosen endeavor.

I've always had an innate drive and an intensity that has driven my success. I don't even remember my 21st birthday, not because I was drunk but because it didn't particularly mean anything to me. I just wanted to work and be successful. Maybe you don't agree that that's a particularly wonderful trait. But it's a trait that is shared by most people who become mega-successful.

So, let's review some of the key points from the book (in no particular order of importance).

Money is made in the buy.

You have to be in the right place at the right time—and act.

You make your own luck.

Get educated. Do your homework.

Find a great business partner.

Find mentors.

You don't have to be first; just build a better mousetrap.

Work with winners—and build a team.

Invest in real estate.

Own your own property.

Seek rental income.

Don't burn bridges.

Dress for success.

Don't be a quitter.

Embrace failure.

Know your strengths and your weaknesses.

Exceed expectations.

Be the best in breed.

Get healthy. Stay healthy.

Spend your money wisely.

Don't get in debt.

Help others; give back

THE END

132 Make It Happen

133 Make It Happen

www.ingramcontent.com/pod-product-compliance
Lightning Source LLC
Chambersburg PA
CBHW032005190326
41520CB00007B/365